THE ANATOMY OF CAPTIVITY

THE
ANATOMY OF CAPTIVITY

John Laffin

ABELARD-SCHUMAN
London   New York   Toronto

WARNER MEMORIAL LIBRARY
EASTERN COLLEGE
ST. DAVIDS, PA.   19087

BY THE SAME AUTHOR:

War and Military history:

Middle East Journey
Return to Glory
One Man's War
Digger (Story of the Australian
  Soldier)
Scotland the Brave (Story of the
  Scottish Soldier)
Jackboot (Story of the German
  Soldier)
Face of War
British Campaign Medals
Codes and Ciphers
The Walking Wounded
Anzacs at War
Boys in Battle
Links of Leadership
Tommy Atkins (Story of the
  English Soldier)
Women in Battle

General:

The Hunger to Come (The Food
  and Population Crises)
Crime and Adventure
Jungle Manhunt
The Devil's Emissary
The Dance of San Jose
Murder on Flight 354
Murder by Bamboo
I'll Die Tonight
Death has my Number
Crime on my Hands
My Brother's Executioner
Doorways to Danger
New Geography 1966–67

© Copyright 1968 by John Laffin
First published in Great Britain
1968
First published in U.S.A. 1968
L.C.C.C. No. 68–24682
Standard Book Number
200.71528.3

LONDON
Abelard-Schuman
Limited
8 King Street WC 2

NEW YORK
Abelard-Schuman
Limited
6 West 57 Street

TORONTO
Abelard-Schuman
Canada Limited
896 Queen Street West

to Klaus Fluegge

HV 6254 .L3 1968
Laffin, John.
The anatomy of captivity

Contents

Author's Note

This book is built on the ordeals, terrors and indignities suffered by many men and women and because of this and despite the risk of sounding pontifical the author believes that he should warn that the climate under which political captivity is possible is not peculiar to certain countries and that it could easily be produced in those nations which consider themselves bastions of freedom, the United Kingdom and the United States, for example. Indeed, in both these nations some trends towards this climate are already disturbingly evident; the growth of bureaucracy is one of them. The only safe-guards are a free press, a vigorous parliamentary opposition and an alert public. The second two cannot function without the first; the press is the first target of those men who are prepared to do to other men the terrible things narrated in this book.

The spelling of foreign place names varies so much that, where possible, the anglicised version is given.

The Author is grateful to those former political prisoners who have answered so frankly his sometimes personal and intimate questions. As always, he owes much to his wife for the great burden of typing the manuscript and her assistance in research.

Foreword

A dangerous aspect of political captivity is the view of some people that it is history, that it all happened yesterday and that the world is much more enlightened now. In fact, the world has hundreds of thousands of political prisoners; men and women are arrested every day and subjected to the humiliating procedures described in this book. My analysis of captivity concentrates on Europe—because this is where the most reliable information is available—but political imprisonment is virtually world wide.

In 1967 one of the more notorious cases concerned Régis Debray, a twenty-six-year-old French journalist-intellectual kept without trial in a Bolivian prison. Sent to cover the Bolivian guerilla war, Debray was arrested in April in the village of Muyumpampa. The French journal, *Le Monde*, claimed that Debray was merely seeking medical supplies; both French and Latin American newspapers say that he was tortured. Bolivia's president, General Rene Barrientos Ortuna, calls Debray an "adventurer", but his reasons for gaoling the Frenchman are political. Debray is the author of *Revolution in the Revolution?*, a textbook for Latin American revolutionaries, which has given him a following of Bolivian students.

Pressure put on the Bolivian government by the Pope, General de Gaulle and many writers and intellectuals had no apparent result, though it may, in fact, have kept Debray from the firing squad. Prisoners in Bolivia with less influential friends have been tortured and killed.

In 1967 the Supreme Court of Brazil ordered a book to be released which had been banned by the Minister of Justice when it first appeared in 1966. The book, *Torturas e Torturados* by Marcio Moreira Alves, gives details of imprisonments and various methods of torture inflicted on political prisoners under the regime of President Castelo Branco.

Very little documentary evidence is available about other South American countries but *The Times* of February 14th, 1968 reported that in Paraguay there are about 150 political prisoners who have been incarcerated for years without trial under the regime of President Stoessner.

9

In the Soviet Union in 1967 friends of a political prisoner could help him no more than they could in earlier years, as is clear from the case of Julij Danielj, who in June was sentenced to five years' forced labour for having had his writings published in the West, a purely political "crime". His wife was permitted to visit the camp, 350 miles from Moscow, but then obstacles were put in her way. She was restricted to visiting the camp for one hour—although her original permit granted her three days—visiting hours were changed and she was not permitted to carry food.

Writing to the Soviet government, Mrs. Danielj complained that the prison authorities refused to allow her husband to use mosquito-repellent, though mosquitoes were rife. When he protested he was badly beaten and thrown into the camp cells. Danielj was in ill-health—partly as a result of severe war injuries—but he was not allowed to lie down during the day, a standard rule in the prison. Listing many punishments meted out to prisoners, Mrs. Danielj said that the life and health of a prisoner were in the hands of a commandant, instructor or guard, all of whom were quick to find fault.

Mrs. Danielj also wrote to the President and Secretariat of the Writers' Union but had no acknowledgment and believes that her letter, which the Union passed on to the authorities, brought punishment to her husband. The government went through the motions of holding an inquiry into Mrs. Danielj's allegations but dismissed them as "completely unfounded". The commission noted that "the living and working conditions in the camp correspond exactly with the regulations".

This is no doubt the case in Greece, where trials by military tribunals are held in secret. As late as October 1967 an estimated 3,000 political offenders were in prison, but this figure conceals the continual terror, for political gaols have a changing population. Between April 21, 1967, the day of the Greek military coup, and the end of October about 40,000 people had been arrested.

The confession rate was high because many of the people arrested were elderly and infirm and more easily convinced that "confession" would be less painful than insistence on innocence. The names of many had been on police lists ever since the civil war of 1947-49, when they had been branded as disloyal. As will be seen in this book, it is next to impossible for authority to acknowledge that a man or woman accused of political subversion, instability, un-

10

reliability or irresponsibility could possibly have changed his views.

A bus conductor was charged with having "insulted the army" because he challenged a soldier who refused to pay his fare.* The conductor now has the beginnings of a dossier as a political offender. A "suspicious friendship" is enough to give a person a bad name, while personal influence, as a youth-club leader for example, gives him a worse one. There is even such a thing as "precautionary arrest"—just in case a person might become a political offender.

In Spain there are, officially, about 1,500 political prisoners, but some more realistic reports claim 30,000. They go before the Special Public Order Courts which enforce harsh laws with severe penalties. Victims come from all opposition groups—students, socialists, Basque nationalists, carriers of prohibited literature. Portugal has between 200 and 350 political prisoners. One of the more prominent was Jose Vitoriano, now 50, who spent sixteen years in gaols. First arrested in 1948 on charges of spreading subversive propaganda he was in prison for three years. Re-arrested in 1953 he was badly ill-treated and given another four years. As his sentence expired he was re-arrested on a charge of plotting against the state while inside a prison camp. After another five years he was released in 1966, but he cannot expect to remain free.

Occasionally people under trial for political "offences" have the immense courage to stand up in court and try to explain what has been happening to them. Even in the Soviet Union men and women are finding the bravery necessary to dare to challenge the might of the state. Such gestures will in time bring their reward. But let nobody think that political captivity is history. It is still making history.

---

* Mervyn Jones, in the *New Statesman*, October 20, 1967.

11

About the Captives

The more prominent political prisoners whose experiences are detailed in this book are referred to only by their surnames, so brief biographical notes about each of them are given here. The five exceptions are Dreyfus, Trenck, "A.D.", Nolan and Orsini, whose careers are described in separate chapters.

BEAUSOBRE, IULIA DE. One of the most interesting captives of modern times, Mrs. de Beausobre and her husband had plenty of opportunity after the Russian Revolution broke out in 1917 to leave Russia, live elsewhere and adopt a new nationality; many of their countrymen did just this. The de Beausobres thought they had something to give Russia and preferred to "stand by" her; for ten years they served the Soviet state. On February 4, 1932 they were suddenly and unaccountably arrested; Mrs. de Beausobre was interned for nine months in Moscow and for a third of this time was in solitary. Later she was moved to another prison and found herself in the company of women thieves, prostitutes and drug addicts. Five years in a prison camp followed this. She never again heard of her husband.

BEGIN, MENACHEM. One of the leading Jews in Poland, Begin emigrated to Lithuania in 1940, He was arrested that year by the Russians and charged with being "an enemy of the people". He was sentenced to eight years imprisonment, but was released after three, as Poland was by then an ally of Russia. One of the founders of modern Israel, Begin is also one of the great freedom fighters of the century.

BETTELHEIM, BRUNO. Born in Vienna in 1903, this psychologist was imprisoned in the prison camps of Dachau and Buchenwald before the war and on release went to the United States. He is Professor of Educational Psychology at the University of Chicago.

His book, *The Informed Heart*, is a profound and dispassionate account of men's behaviour as prisoners of the SS.

BLUMBERG, MYRNA (Mrs. Kenneth Mackenzie). Born in Africa in 1935, Miss Blumberg spent some years in England before returning to Cape Town as the wife of a journalist. She was the Cape Town correspondent for the *Daily Herald*. A woman of liberal political views she was arrested a few weeks after the shooting of Dr. Verwoerd in April, 1960. No reason was given for her arrest. She was taken away from her small daughter and husband and imprisoned for some months without a trial.

BONE, EDITH. Born in Budapest in 1889, Dr. Bone became a Communist and for some years lived and worked in Russia. Fluent in six languages—she learnt a seventh, Greek, in gaol—she lived in several European countries including England. When she returned to Hungary in 1949 she was arrested, though by then she was a British subject, and gaoled for "having been engaged in espionage for England". An indomitable woman, Dr. Bone managed, despite her age and the treatment to which she was subjected, to impose her will on her captors. Her book, *Seven Years Solitary*, is one of the finest accounts of political captivity ever written.

BONNIVARD. Born in 1496 and a great liberal of his day, Bonnivard in 1523 so irritated the Duke of Savoy through his efforts to free the Genevese from the burden of Savoyard rule, that the Duke put him into the dungeons of the Castle of Grolee for two years. Failing to learn his lesson, Bonnivard again took up politics and again, in 1530, fell into the Duke of Savoy's hands. He was taken secretly to the dungeons of Chillon, on the edge of Lake Geneva, and here he languished while his relations and friends wondered if he was still alive.

BURNEY, CHRISTOPHER. An Englishman, Burney spent eighteen months in solitary confinement, as a prisoner of the Nazis. His book, *Solitary Confinement*, is notable for Burney's account of his search for spiritual guidance and comfort and for the frankness, honesty and sincerity of his reflections.

CISZEK, FATHER WALTER J. Born in Pennsylvania in 1904 of Polish parents, Walter Ciszek became a Jesuit priest. Specially trained for evangelical work, he entered Russia with a group of Polish refugees in 1939, but two years later was arrested as "a spy of the Vatican". He spent fifteen years in gaols and labour camps and another eight years free but restricted, during which time he worked as a priest. In October, 1963, he was exchanged for a Russian spy held by the Americans and returned to the United States. His book, *With God in Russia*, provides an unusual insight into the workings of the Soviet penal system.

EKART, ANTONI. Born in Warsaw in 1912, Ekart was educated as an engineer in Poland and Switzerland. When war broke out in 1939 he was ordered to east Poland, where he was caught in the Russian invasion. Ekart tried to take his sick wife to relative safety in Lithuania but they were caught by the Russians. Both were imprisoned, Ekart being sentenced to three years for various nonsensical and uncommitted crimes. In fact, he stayed in captivity for nearly eight years before his wife, who had returned to Poland earlier, was able to agitate sufficiently to cause the puppet government in Warsaw to ask for his release. Now living in Sweden, Ekart believes that in 1947 he was the only inhabitant of the Soviet slave state who managed to get through the iron curtain—one out of thirty million.

FRANKL, VIKTOR. An Austrian psychiatrist and psychotherapist, Dr. Frankl was a prisoner of the Nazis in Auschwitz, Dachau and other prison camps. A man of international reputation, Dr. Frankl is most noted for his logotherapy, a school of existential psychiatry which focuses on the patient's future rather than his past. (Logos = reason, *Greek*). A basic tenet of logotherapy is that man's main concern is not to gain pleasure or to avoid pain but to see a meaning in his life. Application of his own theory helped to bring Dr. Frankl through his prison ordeals.

HEIMLER, EUGENE. An Hungarian Jew, Heimler was born in 1922 and survived periods in four Nazi concentration camps. A man of high intellect and great determination he emigrated to England in 1947 and qualified as a psychiatric social worker in 1953. He is regarded as one of the pioneers of community mental health, a subject in which he is qualified by experience as well as by training. He has written two biographical books.

IGNOTUS, PAUL. This Hungarian was a refugee in London during World War II and became Press Secretary at the Hungarian Legation afterwards. In 1949, on a visit to Budapest, he was arrested by the AVO. (State Security Department) and remained their prisoner, suffering every kind of hardship, for seven years. He re-

15

turned to London on his release, bringing with him his wife, who had been a prisoner in the same gaol. His book, *Political Prisoner*, is a level-headed, dispassionate account of life in Hungarian prisons.

KOESTLER, ARTHUR. Multi-lingual, a brilliant journalist and novelist, Koestler ran foul of Franco's troops in Malaga in 1937 and was imprisoned first in Malaga and then in Seville. His book, *Dialogue With Death*, an account of his experiences, is possibly the wisest in the literature of political captivity and should be read by all students of the subject.

LANCE, CHRISTOPHER. Born in 1893, Lance served in World War I, and won the D.S.O. After service in Russia in 1919 he worked as an engineer in South America and Spain. High-spirited, quixotic, a champion of the underdog, Lance became "the Spanish Pimpernel". During the war years of 1936-37 he successfully smuggled out of Spain nearly one hundred men and women who faced death if caught. Through the carelessness and ingratitude of one of these people, Lance himself was caught and imprisoned. He suffered acutely in seven Republican prisons for sixteen months and narrowly escaped death. The night before his execution he was driven to the border and freedom, the result of political intervention. He never fully recovered from the torment inflected upon him.

LEISNER, FATHER KARL. Born on February 28, 1915, at Rees on the lower Rhine, Karl Leisner was brought up in Cleve. He became interested in the Catholic Youth Movement and travelled through much of Europe in connection with this organisation. After a compulsory period in the youth labour service, he became a student of theology in Munster. In February, 1939, he was ordained a sub-deacon and in March consecrated as deacon. Ill in a sanatorium in November, 1939, Leisner was one of a group of patients discussing the attempt on Hitler's life in the Munich beer cellar. Hearing that many people had been killed, Leisner said to himself, "Too bad the Fuhrer was not there." He believed that Hitler himself had organised the incident and meant that had he been present much suffering would have been avoided. Fanatics among the patients reported him for his indiscretion and he was summarily arrested. As a leader of Catholic Youth he was, in any case, a political "enemy of the German people". After surviving five and half years in captivity he died a few months after his release from Dachau.

LEVI, PRIMO. An Italian Jew, Levi was born in Turin in 1919. A

16

chemist with a university degree, he ran foul of the Nazis and was deported to Auschwitz in 1944. He was one of the very few Auschwitz prisoners to survive the war. His book, *If This Is a Man*, is one of the most perceptive and moving books in all prison literature.

LIPPER, ELINOR. Born in Brussels in 1912 of German-Jewish parents, Miss Lipper became a Communist while a medical student in Berlin in the 1930s. After the rise of Hitler she went to Italy and in 1937 took a job in Moscow. Within two months she was arrested in the "Great Purge" and sentenced to five years' imprisonment for "counter-revolutionary activities". The sentence was lengthened to eleven years of Siberian slavery; she was not released until 1948. In ten different prisons and fourteen prison camps, Miss Lipper had ample opportunity to observe prison life and her book, *Eleven Years in Soviet Prison Camps*, provides probably the most detailed account available of day to day life.

MALSAGOFF, S. A. After serving with the White Russian armies in the campaigns following World War I, Malsagoff surrendered to the Communists after their offer of complete amnesty. But he was arrested and imprisoned in the notorious Solovetsky Islands in the White Sea, where at least a quarter of a million prisoners were murdered. Malsagoff escaped in 1925 and found sanctuary in Finland.

MONTPENSIER, DUC DE (Antoine Philippe d'Orléans). At the age of seventeen this French nobleman was arrested by the Revolutionaries in April, 1793, and spent forty-three months in Fort St. Jean prison, Marseilles. His younger brother was gaoled at the same time, but had less rigorous conditions. Their father was taken from the same gaol to his execution. Montpensier told much of his own story in his memoirs and in personal letters, together translated by Malcolm Hay in *Prince in Captivity*.

PALOCZI-HORVATH, GEORGE. Born in 1908, of parents from the Hungarian Calvinist nobility, Paloczi-Horvath led an active, eventful and intellectual life. Escaping from Hungary in 1941, he served with the British Special Operations Executive. In 1947 he returned to his country, joined the Communist Party and was made head of the Foreign Language Department of Hungarian radio and of the Hungarian Broadcasting and News Agency. In 1949, for reasons never divulged, he was arrested and imprisoned. During his five years in gaol he had plenty of time to become disillusioned with the

Communist system. Released in 1954, he escaped to the West during the Hungarian Revolution of 1956. His book, *The Undefeated*, gives an excellent account of how the big "purge" trials are prepared.

PARVILAHTI, UNTO. A Finn. Born in 1907, Parvilahti, an aerial photographer and cartographer, fought against the Russians in 1939-40, then with the Germans against the Russians. After the armistice between Finland and the Soviet Union in 1944 he was kidnapped by the Secret Police for "anti-Communist activities", and after imprisonment in Helsinki was handed over to the Russians.

PELLICO, SILVIO, Born at Saluzzo in Piedmont in 1789, Pellico was a successful poet and playwright before he turned publisher of the newspaper *Il Conciliatore*. Initiated into the Carbonari revolutionary movement, he was arrested in 1820 and imprisoned, mostly in the Spielberg, where he suffered acutely. In 1832 he wrote *Le mie prigioni—My Prisons*.

RUPERT, RAPHAEL. This Hungarian lawyer, imprisoned for nine years in the Soviet Union, is one of the most dispassionate witnesses about the facts of political captivity. He was an underground worker for the Allies during World War II, and helped Britons, Jews, Dutch and Hungarians to escape from German hands. In Vienna after the war he was given a minor and quite open temporary job at British Headquarters; it was this which led to the Russians accusing him of being a British spy. An idealist and politically naive, Rupert returned to Budapest in the summer of 1947 where he was arrested and handed over to the Russians. Repatriated to Hungary in November 1955, as an act of clemency, Rupert was still considered guilty of crimes against the Soviet Union. When he arrived in Hungary he was re-arrested by his own people. For several months he was imprisoned in a former Carmelite Convent and was then transferred to Budapest, where he spent more months in the prison hospital. Rupert escaped to Austria during the Hungarian Revolution of October-November 1956.

SCHOLMER, JOSEPH. Born in 1912, Scholmer was a doctor in Germany but became a member of the Communist Party and was imprisoned by the Nazis. In 1949 he was arrested by the East Germans and as an "enemy of the people" was sentenced to twenty-five years' imprisonment in Siberia. He was released in 1953 during the thaw which followed Stalin's death.

TURNER, HENRY. This Englishman, an officer of the R.A.F.and

Air Attaché in Warsaw, 1947-49, tried to smuggle out of Poland a girl with whom he had fallen in love. At this time he was no longer a Foreign Office employee and had resigned his commission. He and the girl were caught and imprisoned. Turner was accused of having been involved in espionage while Air Attaché and in due course he "confessed". He accepted the Poles' offer of asylum in Poland and lived happily for a time with his sweetheart. Later he asked for permission to return to England and was re-arrested. Released some months later and ordered to leave Poland, he reversed his intentions and asked permission to stay. It was refused and Turner left behind him the girl he had compromised.

THOMSEN, ALEXANDER. A Dane, born in 1917, Thomsen lost both parents at the age of six. He won a medical degree at the University of Kiel, Germany, and later became a Red Cross doctor. After the fall of Berlin he went to that city where he helped Scandinavians trapped there. "Invited" to return to Denmark via Moscow, Thomsen was arrested; months later he learned that he was supposed to have helped Nazi fugitives to escape justice. His own government and that of Sweden as well as various Red Cross organisations failed to help him and in some cases disowned him. Released after ten years' imprisonment in Arctic regions, Dr. Thomsen had to fight to clear his name in his own country; however, he was able to extricate from the Soviet Union the woman prisoner-doctor with whom he had fallen in love and who had borne his son.

VRBA, DR. RUDOLPH. Born in Czechoslovakia in 1924, Vrba was arrested and gaoled in Auschwitz and Maidanek. Escaping from Auschwitz in 1944—a rare feat—he joined a Czechoslovak partisan unit and won three awards for bravery. After postwar study in Prague he emigrated to England in 1960 and has lived there ever since. He is an authority in neurochemistry. His book, *I Cannot Forgive*, has been described as "one of the most terrible documents ever penned". Vrba's observant eyes and his memory for detail expose all the savagery of the SS prison system.

WELLS, LEON WELICZKER. A Polish Jew, Wells was imprisoned by the Nazis at the age of sixteen. He twice escaped from Janowska Prison, where he endured incredible hardship. He was the only member of his family to survive the war; his parents, two brothers and four sisters disappeared. His book, *The Janowska Road*, is a cold indictment of Nazi cruelty to the Jews.

1

The Phenomenon

☗☗☗☗☗☗☗☗☗☗☗☗☗☗

Man's inhumanity to man is now so commonplace, and apparently so accepted as inevitable, that it rouses little anger except among poets and humanitarians. Yet in a world which has become so civilised, so progressive, so clever and so educated, political detainees are still treated abominably. In no pursuit has Man shown such inventiveness, ingenuity and assiduity as in tormenting his political enemies. The political prisoner may not always be kept in filthy conditions and his creature comforts may sometimes be better than in former times, but science and the mind of man have devised for him torments, stresses and indignities that the Inquisition never even dreamed of. It is almost as if Man reserves the worst of his spleen for this particular enemy, as if he is not prepared to grant him any rights at all.

The political loses his dignity as well as his honour; he becomes the outsider, the scapegoat. This enforced role lends a peculiar fascination to the stories of prisoners. It is not so much physical suffering, the ordeal of pain and torture, the fear of terrible death or the inevitable inadequacy of the description of bodily pain that grips the imagination; it is the loss of human dignity and the feeling that "there but for the Grace of God . . . " Human dignity is not altogether abstract; it is made up, in part, of love and companionship, and of personal taste in such little things as choice of toothpaste and soap. Deprived of these things a man is damaged just as surely as by a kick in the kidneys.

Suddenly taken out of the mainstream of life, a political prisoner is pushed into a stagnant offshoot where there is no movement. We take a lot for granted in normal life and most of it is trivia, the thousands of little commonplaces that make up day-to-day life. Some of it is deliberate action, such as setting out to buy a list of household and personal wants; much of it is chance, such as meeting a friend and having a drink with him, or receiving in the mail a letter detailing some unexpected opportunity. Much of what we take for granted is simple choice: to stay home and watch television or read a book, or to go to the cinema or pub; to buy X or Z brand of petrol; to seek the company of Helga or Hilda; or to take out another insurance policy with A company or B company. A man does not realise how much choice he has in life until he is deprived of it. In captivity all this goes—the chance, the trivial, the vital, the deliberate. In prison everything is ordained, ordered and imposed. Without the ability to make choices of any kind, the captive feels small, impotent and unimportant—a mere thing to be moved inertly and unresistantly about.

This book is an attempt to trace the anatomy of political captivity, and to understand some of its causes and effects. I have exercised the discretion of an author to depart slightly from my own terms of reference to include a few people who were not, strictly speaking, political captives pure and simple. Some historians might put Dreyfus into the treason category. But he was not guilty of treason and it is now clear that he was a victim of a political conspiracy.

It is important that humanity and society—which are not quite the same thing—should know the anatomy of captivity because, as the world moves into the computer age, the number of political captives grows. A time could come when every individualist will face the danger of imprisonment if he speaks, acts or even thinks in a way contrary to the omniscient and omnipotent Big Brother. Frankl, an outstandingly perceptive and educated political prisoner, believes that "More and more he [man] will be governed by what others want him to do, thus increasingly falling prey to conformism."

Political captives of every era have known about Big Brother. Call it what you will—the Inquisition, the Gestapo, the NKD. or the Cheka, the State Police or any one of a score of other names—it is the same super-sensitive, easily offended being of corporate conscience, so ready to dog, denounce, damn and destroy.

"Arbitrary power has introduced the whip of slavery, and the mechanic subordination has eradicated these noble and rational incitements to concord and harmony. Instead of these mistrust and slavish fear have arisen, the enthusiastic spirit of the Brandenburg warrior declines and into this error have most of the European states fallen." So wrote Trenck in 1792 after his long captivity.

A century and a half later Nehru, himself a political prisoner, wrote, "In prison one comes to realise more than anywhere else the basic nature of the state; it is the force, the compulsion, the violence of the governing group. It always seems curious to me how the governing group in a state, basing itself on an extremity of violence, objects on moral or ethical grounds to the force or violence of others . . . "

George Washington was as blunt about authority. "Government is not reason, it is not eloquence—it is force! Like fire, it is a dangerous servant and a fearful master."

A political prisoner is punished not so much for what he has done but for what he represents. This is why during a purge the gaols become full of scientists, professors, generals and men in high social positions; such men are a potential threat to the system of acceptable beliefs.

Authority objects not only to conclusions which run counter to the Establishment; it objects to an individual who thinks at all, especially if he is given to transmitting thoughts into action. Stock and Reynolds pointed out in 1938 that Quakers and Communists, atheists and Plymouth Brethren, were "all delivered at Wormwood Scrubs under one common label, because Authority had declared it from a certain date a moral duty to kill Germans [at the outbreak of war in 1914], just as surely as Authority would have hanged any one of these men for killing a German before the day war was declared."

Ancient states, stifled in superstition, demanded human sacrifices. Modern states, imbued with intolerance, still demand them. The main differences are that modern victims far outnumber the ancient ones, and they are far more brutally treated than those of former times. Indeed, it is clear that the indignities, humiliations and bestialities inflicted on political prisoners have been worsening century by century. Political prisoners have existed from the time

23

that one group of men, hungry for power, felt itself threatened by a group with contrary views. The dominant power has changed little over the centuries; monarchs, princes, dukes, dictators have all imprisoned their enemies. Various religions, including Christianity, have, in the name of holiness, doomed and deep-dungeoned countless sceptics and unbelievers. Now it is the "state" which incarcerates "the enemies of the people". These "enemies" are often people of the same race, which makes the phenomenon of political captivity all the more complex.

One of the most extraordinary facets of the anatomy of captivity is that many of the men who bring others to the hell of prison do so in good faith in the belief that they are doing only what is just. At any rate they succeed in rationalising their behaviour: the prime examples are those learned judges who sentenced the Nazis' prisoners. They had an eye on their own survival, but there can be no doubt that many had a genuine belief in the law as the Nazis demanded that it be imposed. However, I have found only one captive who has conceded that authority could be just. This is the Italian Pellico who, despite his anguish at a sentence of fifteen years, asks himself, "And who are you, wretched mortal, to claim the right not to be judged with severity by any of your fellow men?"

But forgiveness of his enemies did not prevent Pellico from writing an account of his judgment and punishment. In Kotlas prison camp, in Russia, Antoni Ekart saw scrawled in rusty liquid on the walls of a latrine, "May he be damned who, after regaining freedom, remains silent". Recollection of this invocation helped to inspire Ekart to commit his experiences to paper. Nobody who values the dignity of man can remain silent about the ordeals of political prisoners.

In the twentieth century there is no such thing as a political captive "type", nor is there a particular age bracket. Malsagoff, a prisoner in the Solovetsky Islands in the White Sea in 1925 knew a captive aged 110 and forty other very old men from the Trans-Caucasian Republic. They were political hostages for their sons, grandsons and great-grandsons who were at that time in hiding from the Cheka.

Edith Bone was awarded fifteen years "in solitary confinement with total isolation", an appalling sentence for an unwell woman in her sixties. But in Budapest Central Prison in 1956 she knew of an old woman prisoner who was paralysed and could neither speak nor write nor move. She was kept in gaol because of crimes supposedly committed by members of her family. In Butirka in 1946 a prominent prisoner was Prince Sergei Obolensky, a much-weakened eighty-two. In 1940 Menachem Begin had a cell neighbour aged 78, nearly blind and deaf and so weak that his comrades had to carry him to the lavatory. He had been arrested and gaoled because, in 1914, he had served the Czar and was, therefore, an "enemy of the people".

On the other hand Svetlana Tukhachevska, daughter of an army marshal, was only eleven years old when her father was executed. The NKVD waited until she was seventeen to sentence her to five years in gaol as a "socially dangerous element," in that she was the daughter of her father.

Another phenomenon of political captivity is that so many men inflict it on others and that so many of the victims survive it. In 1884, an English traveller, Charles Cook, stated that European Russia had 73,796 political prisoners. Prychodko claims that in 1939 and 1940 no fewer than 15,000,000 were held in Russian concentration camps. A year after the war ended, there were more than 45,000,000 prisoners or deportees in the Soviet Union; about 15,000,000 of them were foreigners.

Captivity is as difficult to eradicate as war and prostitution, and it suffers in comparison with them, for they can be talked about openly. A war, indeed, is one of the few things that *cannot* be hidden. It involves many people and makes much noise, and though at times there have been rulers and nations who have wanted to hush up a war, campaign or battle, they have never succeeded in doing so. Prostitution, by its very nature, is as much public property as the bodies of its practitioners. Although societies have sometimes pretended not to see it, they have always been aware of it, and from time to time outraged or enraged public opinion has forced governments to act. But captivity is private, personal and without publicity.

The political prisoner is not allowed to make any noise and since the government or ruler has been responsible for his imprisonment he cannot expect authority to be interested in his release. Until recently no organised body existed to take any notice of the plight of the political prisoner.

A prisoner-of-war is more fortunate in enduring a reasonable form of captivity, at least in modern times. The British, American, Australian, German and Italian servicemen taken prisoner by one another found boredom their chief torment. If they obeyed the camp rules they were not molested, and were adequately fed, clothed and even protected. The Russians and Germans maltreated each other as prisoners and the barbarities and cruelties perpetrated by the Japanese on their military prisoners have stamped themselves into history. Still, it is true to say that the vast number of military prisoners had no real grounds for complaint against their captors.

The political detainee is not so fortunate. It would be as well here to define, for purposes of this book, the term political prisoner. The word "political" seems to imply that the person concerned has an interest in politics, but often this is not the case. For example many if not most of the Jews imprisoned, tortured and executed by the Nazis had no real political convictions but they were political captives in the sense that a political force incarcerated them. The political detainee has usually committed no crime against society or the common law, but has somehow offended, or allegedly offended, the state, be it in the person of a ruler or high official or the government. In many cases there has been neither offence nor intent to offend. There are cases of men and women who have spent many years in captivity without ever knowing what they were accused of. Others have been aware of the charge but have been innocent of it— and often the person responsible for putting them into a cell has known of their innocence.

A civil prisoner usually knows how long he must spend in prison, be it a month or twenty years or life. The political detainee, however, faces an indeterminate sentence; this is one of his greatest tortures. The civil prisoner once lived in foul squalor, but generally he had company; many political prisoners have had the foulness without the company. In more modern times civil prisoners in ordinary gaols have had many privileges, such as mail and visits from their family. In Britain there have been cases of convicts allowed out to indulge in drinking parties with their wives. One man left gaol, travelled some miles by taxi and bought a budgerigar.

In Sweden civil prisoners have countless amenities and privileges— supremely comfortable rooms with hot and cold water, television, ornaments and pictures, private visits from wives in the privacy of their own "cells", three-course meals, training in some trade or craft, money when they leave gaol.

Military prisoners have no such luxury, but their families generally know in what prison camp they are kept, and are able to send them letters and parcels. The political prisoner often does not know where he is held and his relatives are not informed. He has no mail, no visits, no privileges of any kind. He is a forgotten man.

Even men and women directly convicted of espionage and treason, though they sometimes spend long terms in captivity, live under better conditions than the purely political captive, who is subject to the strictest security precautions. It is rare for a political prisoner even to attempt an escape, for no matter how vast a country may be, there is no hiding place for a political. It is too dangerous for anybody to harbour him.

Whichever way one regards them, political prisoners suffer more than others. Throughout the ages men have been cruel to their captives, whether military, civil or political. But the refinements of cruelty have been reserved for the political detainee. Whereas a civil prisoner guilty of petty theft in 1750 was put in the stocks and pelted with refuse, the man accused of political offence was put on the rack and stretched until his joints cracked. A captured soldier might have had to endure boredom, hunger and cold before he was exchanged or before he enlisted in his captor's army, but he was rarely maltreated.

It is popularly supposed, on the principle that where there is smoke there must be at least a little fire, that every political prisoner has "brought it on himself", or that "he has asked for it". This is demonstrably not so in many cases, though in some instances a prisoner has finished in a cell because of pride, which prevented him from escaping when the danger was obvious, or prejudice which has made him indiscreet to the point of stupidity and antagonised an enemy beyond pacifying.

If we leave out of reckoning the vast numbers of people imprisoned by the Nazis and the Russians it is clear that no one nation has infamy of place as a captor. Ironically, some of those countries which pride themselves on qualities such as liberty, equality and fraternity are among the most enthusiastic and brutal captors.

The scope of "security precautions" makes everybody vulnerable. In some Communist countries there is a "cadre file" about every citizen which contains more information than most of the subjects would credit. The file will contain the subject's school record, including copies of teachers' estimates of character and ability, his

27

work record, with particular reference to anything "reactionary" or "inflammatory" that he may have said, records of denunciations made by neighbours, workmates, personnel supervisors, party officials, notes on gossip picked up from every conceivable source. Even the books the subject may borrow from a library are noted in his dossier. Later all this may be brought out and used in evidence against the subject; it is never used *for* him. Suppose that some time in his career he makes a mistake in a blueprint or a column of figures or in a machine part he is making; should he run foul of the Security Police, this error may be assessed as sabotage or as indication that he is unreliable.

The great claw of political captivity has never groped so far for new victims. A political system that cannot hold its people by the more conventional and traditional methods of persuasion must resort to force. In Hungary in 1952 batches of prisoners were thrown into gaols almost every day. "Political" only by tortuous deviations of the definition, they included peasants with more than twenty acres of land who refused to join collective farms, former landowners, bank employees, clerical workers denounced as "Fascists", and self-employed men, such as shoe repairers, who refused to join a union.

In June, 1940, many Russians were gaoled for arriving late at work by twenty minutes or more; changing one's place of work without permission was also a prison offence. The 100,000 soldiers who had been captured by the Finns during the war of 1940, the so-called winter war, were arrested as political prisoners when they returned home and were punished for "betraying" their country by allowing themselves to be captured; vast numbers were shot, and a certain proportion of every hundred were gaoled as "enemies of the people".

The treatment of political prisoners depends much on direction from the top. In Hungary between 1945 and 1950 prisoners were treated humanely once they reached gaol, though they may have been roughly handled during interrogations. The sane and reasonable treatment during that period was the policy the Minister of Justice, Dr. Reis. The changeover to brutality came almost overnight when the AVH. men took over the gaols from the Ministry of Justice. They inspected the prisons and beat nearly half of the captives, merely to establish their authority. The political prisoner in Communist lands has this special right: to be hungrier than the hungry, more debased than the lowliest.*

One obstacle to improving the treatment of prisoners is the gullibility of well intentioned people invited to inspect prisons. Such inspections take place periodically in several countries, usually to calm agitation. Members of the parliament, political leaders, Red Cross delegates, churchmen and others have all been deluded into thinking that "conditions are not so bad after all". Authority goes to great trouble to give this impression, rather in the way that a military unit is prepared for a general's inspection. A particular part of a prison is set apart for the inspection; here cells are cleaned and scrubbed, prisoners are allowed to wash and shave and are issued with comfortable clothing. Furniture is sometimes moved into the cells and evidence is planted to indicate that the captives are reasonably fed and have means of recreation. It is possible to achieve much by showing visitors large amounts of food allegedly left by prisoners so well fed that they could afford to leave crusts of bread, the skins of rice puddings and the stalks of cauliflower. The sight of sports equipment left discreetly in a prison yard is enough to convince an inspection party that prisoners are allowed to keep fit. Reading material is placed in strategic places and signs go up on doors—READING ROOM, WRITING ROOM, LAUNDRY, STORE ROOM, LIBRARY. Sometimes the visitors are allowed to speak with prisoners, sometimes without an officer being present. This is taken to indicate that all is fair, and that prisoners can speak freely. The prisoners on display are usually the trusties, who can be depended on to give the right answers, or ordinary captives who have been briefed for the interview. The briefing is straightforward: "If you say anything critical we will beat you into pulp or give you three months in solitary or your family will suffer." So the prisoner smiles at the well-dressed, well-fed visitor and says, "No, I have no complaints." Even intelligent, professional observers have been tricked in this way, as was veteran journalist Sefton Delmer when he met Christopher Lance aboard the Spanish prison ship in Barcelona Harbour.

Early in his captivity on Devil's Island Alfred Dreyfus wrote in his diary, "My conscience . . . my reason told me each day that the truth at last must burst forth triumphant. In a century like ours

* Begin's expression.

the light cannot be long suppressed; but alas, each day brought a fresh disappointment. The light not only did not break forth, but everything was done to prevent it appearing." Most political prisoners have felt this way. Though they may live for years in hope of release, at heart they eventually come to know that very few people will do anything to help them. In a totalitarian country the chances of help are remote indeed, for the family and friends of a captive run great risks in agitating on his behalf. There is an uncertain point at which intercession becomes dangerous; authority, becoming irritated, may gaol the pleader. In the case of a foreign national, the chance of help is dependent on the political situation and the humanity of officials at home. The government of one country is reluctant to interfere in the domestic affairs of another, even to save one of its own nationals.

Private individuals, without some sort of backing or influence, have little chance of bringing about better conditions or release for a prisoner. This is why the Amnesty organisation is so important as the only effective way of embarrassing political power. It can stir conscience and impart reason. The "reason" may be nothing more than publicity unwelcome to the oppressive authority, but this is often reason enough to bring about release. Justice, as Dreyfus found, cannot be left to itself.

On January 21, 1895 he wrote to his wife: " . . . But what am I asking for night and day? Justice! Justice! Is this the nineteenth century, or have we gone back some hundred years? Is it possible that innocence is not recognised in an age of enlightenment and truth . . . I ask no favour but I ask the justice that is the right of every human being . . . Let those who possess powerful means of investigation use them towards this object; it is for them a sacred duty of humanity and justice . . . "

Dreyfus, like others before and since, still had a blind faith in justice. In all eras political prisoners have said passionately, "Have we gone back to the dark ages?" But the dark ages are continuous; they are always with humanity when political prisoners are concerned. "Is it possible that innocence is not recognised . . . ?" Dreyfus asked. It was the cry of a man who believed that punishment comes only to the wrongdoers. Dreyfus, simple and uncomplicated, had yet to learn that political prisoners are not victims of justice, but of revenge or fear.

2

Arrest: Interrogation: Confession

People charged with offences against common law are usually arrested by day, those accused of political offences by night. The difference is significant and symbolic. Authority is aware that an arrest by night, the taking of a man from the warmth of his family circle, has great shock effect. Also, it is less likely to be witnessed by sympathetic neighbours, who might be roused by the tears of a distraught wife and children. Often the arrest comes as a complete surprise, for the victim knows that he is guilty of no offence. He cannot know that some other victim, further along the chain and under great stress, has given his interrogators some names, *any* names, in an effort to take the pressure from himself. Nearly always, the victim goes quietly. He does not want his family involved and, naively, he believes that there has been some mistake and that he has only to explain the situation. But political arrest is irreversible. For one thing, authority cannot admit that it has made a mistake and for another, no human being is considered important enough to bother about. In any period of extremism, as during the Nazi regime, mistakes often happen. In Vienna, Gestapo officials arrested a man, took him away and shot him, discovered they had grabbed the wrong man, and returned his ashes to his wife.

Once in the net the captive stays there, for no matter what the circumstances no official appears to have the authority to release him. It is only after persistent agitation from many quarters or the onset of a political thaw that he may finally find himself released.

31

The official attitude to arrests is extremely cynical. An NKVD interrogating officer told Ekart in 1939, "The NKVD prefer to arrest a thousand innocent people, if we suspect there is one guilty one among them, rather than to leave the thousand at liberty and let the guilty one be with them." This has been the policy of most other similar police organisations, except where they have specific instructions to bring in some particularly important victim.

There is nothing new in all this. Torquemada, the driving force of the Spanish Inquisition, stated in 1560 that no person would be arrested unless there was good proof of guilt. This meant that people could be arrested *provided the Inquisition considered there was sufficient proof*. When names slipped from the mouths of men and women who were suffering acute agony in the torture chambers, it was considered sufficient proof and reason for arrest.

Authority resorts to all sorts of ruses to avoid making an arrest at a man's home. It is often much better tactics to create the fiction that a man has gone voluntarily to the police or to some government department connected with it. NKVD agents played hide-and-seek with Begin for ten days. They had decided to arrest him and liquidate him in the usual way and could have done that simply and openly, but they wanted to conceal their real purpose from him. From other prisoners he learnt that he was not the only one whom the NKVD tried to trap by means of a civilian invitation, which does not arouse suspicion. In most cases people went to the various offices to which they were invited, believing that when the matter was "cleared up" they would be allowed to return home. This illusion is useful to authority. If a man is arrested and *knows* that he is arrested, he will seriously doubt the promise that "if you tell the truth you will go home immediately". But a man who is invited for a chat, a man who is requested with all courtesy to reply to a number of questions—why should he not hope that he has prospects of getting out safely? The urge to get out of any police station is very great, but it is nothing compared with the urge to get off NKVD premises. The warrant of arrest, therefore, ostensibly remains in the file. The first interrogation is merely a "chat". And if a man tells the truth, which means if he tells not what he knows but what the NKVD wants him to tell, he will go home to his family.

Authority resorts to all manner of deceit to catch possible political enemies in its net. In October 1924 in Moscow an announcement was made to students who had been excluded from the University on the ground of "bourgeois origin". They were told, "All students excluded from the universities who wish to finish their studies abroad are requested to report on Saturday next at 10.30 a.m. in the courtyard of the Tretjakoff Gallery in order to draw up a joint application for permission to leave the country." Several hundred students attended the rally and found they had walked into a Cheka trap. They were arrested, charged with "suspicious relations with other countries" and locked up. Some were lucky enough to get only three years in gaol; most were sent to prison camps in Siberia.

A roughly similar case was that of Alec Peters, attached to the British military mission in Rumania in 1946. About to set off with his family from the port of Constanza, Peters was asked to come ashore for a few minutes to attend to a few customs formalities. He was arrested and imprisoned.

When an arrest of a "foreign political" character is made, it is usual to conceal the real cause from the public, and to put forward as the reason for the prisoner's arrest some imaginary criminal or civil misdemeanour, quite unconnected with politics. While Popoff, a German citizen, was being daily and hourly cross-examined concerning his "secret counter-revolutionary schemes", the Cheka calmly informed the German Embassy and Popoff's journalistic colleagues that the cause of his arrest was first, "a misunderstanding about his passport", then "suspicious association with Moscow Monarchists", and finally it suggested that it was because of "acts of a criminal nature".

Once the arrest is made the captive has no rights. He usually does not know the precise nature of the charge, being told only that he is "an enemy of the people". He is not permitted to contact a lawyer or his family or friends. From the moment of the arrest he ceases to be an individual.

The pre-interrogation atmosphere during the first few hours of arrest in the cell is shocking and frightening, for the mind is not yet under control and the imagination runs wild. Paloczi-Horvath's experience was typical, after his arrest in September 1949.

Every five minutes the spyhole would crash open and an eye would survey him. He lay down on the plank-bed, his face towards the wall away from the light. He was ordered through the spyhole to lie on his back. Having no pillow, he put his hands under his head. He was told to put his hands palm upwards on the plank so that his wrists were in view in case he should feel like slitting them. Paloczi-Horvath says that a Security Police officer told him, "In this building only we do the killing."

Next morning the prisoners were driven out one by one for a wash, to the lavatory, to get breakfast—a piece of bread and some flour-soup. Various prison formalities. Time passing agonisingly slowly. Then the interrogation, when he was told that a full confession would find authority helpful. Having nothing to confess, Paloczi-Horvath knew not what to do. He was kept awake all night, then had another interview with a different officer. "We know everything about you, you have only to confess." Hours of talking and more sleeplessness. For three weeks he was questioned daily; twice daily he had to type his life story. Everywhere in the building he could hear "screams, groaning, whimpering, sudden shrill shouts".

For the victim the arrest is bad enough; the interrogation can be very harsh. Authority must justify its harsh action to itself; officials cannot admit to themselves that they are browbeating and terrorising helpless and innocent men and women. So they create the fiction that the prisoners are conspirators belonging to some large body of people "dangerous to the state". Having convinced themselves that this is true, they are able to treat the prisoner ruthlessly; he is a dangerous man capable of all sorts of deceits and treacheries. The top level of government encourages officials to feel that in "handling" political captives they are in effect fighting a monstrous conspiracy of evil men. The whole situation becomes self-perpetuating, as the persecutors can find justification for their actions no matter how the prisoner behaves. If he confesses under duress, he has proved that they were right; if he does not confess, he is seen as an even more dangerous and intransigent conspirator.

The significant point, then is that interrogators' questions are not primarily designed to get information but confirmation; that is, "proof" of the presumed guilt of some person, either the prisoner being questioned or some other person.

It is paradoxically true that a close bond is formed between the man who is tortured day in, day out, and the man who, day in and day out, tortures him physically or mentally. It is a closer bond than could possibly exist between the tortured man and a free, unworried citizen. The entire being of tortured and torturer is almost as one and after a time each knows the other as completely as a husband and wife know each other after years of marriage. By "torturer" I do not here mean the routine gaoler, but the official striving to break down his prisoner's mind or body or soul or all three.

An interrogator's merit is assessed according to the number and quality of "confessions" he extracts, therefore he has plenty of incentive to show "enterprise" in his interrogations. Should his results be poor in comparison with those of other interrogators he may find himself without a job or even in a cell of his own.

One of Mrs. de Beausobre's interrogators, with facial bones "strikingly reminiscent of a death's-head", had a gentle approach. Was she warm enough? Too warm? Did she have enough food? Books? He did want her to be comfortable and happy and he was immensely sorry for her difficulties. But in order to be able to help her he must know everything about her. He needed her help for her own benefit. She had lost her only child—he died of hunger in 1919—and seven times, for one reason or another, doctors thought she would die, so she and her husband had decided against other pregnancies. Her interrogator had his own interpretation for her failure to have a second child. "Don't you think our country is good enough for a child of yours to be brought up in?" When she explained her problem, her reluctance to have a child and then perhaps to die and leave her husband to bring up the child, the examiner said, "But surely that is a most bourgeois way of looking at things. *Our* children are so well cared for by the State that all the parents have to do is just to make them."

In no aspect of crime and punishment does the law grind so exceedingly slowly and small as with political prisoners. An inquiry can last for years with frequent lengthy adjournments while further evidence is collected and sifted. Each new fact uncovered about one prisoner is crosschecked against what was known about another prisoner; in this way a large number of people may be incriminated. In the meantime it is not unusual to keep a prisoner in five years solitary confinement.

Isolation is probably a more potent force in extracting a confession than any sort of torture. I do not mean merely physical isolation, though this is often absolute, but the more terrible isolation of intellectual nothingness. It is important in this analysis to consider the effect of this sort of isolation. The man with strong political convictions is prepared to endure much for them, he will even die for them, *provided somebody knows what he has endured and sacrificed.* He needs to know that his voice and example, even if it is only one among millions, will be heard and that he will have helped to overthrow a tyranny. If he knows this, his sufferings have a meaning. In the past most prisoners did know this, for there were reports somewhere or other about their case; perhaps only a short official account of a man's "crime" and punishment. But in modern times authority has made a cult of isolation. Nobody hears what the political "offender" says, nobody learns of his courageous stand, his sacrifice cannot be an example to others. Idealism then seems to have no point. Authority knows very well that once a prisoner is convinced there is no point to his suffering he is beaten. Even the walk to the interrogation room is an ordeal and the Russians take extraordinary care to ensure that no one prisoner catches sight of another. In Lubianka, for instance, the passageways are intricately arranged and at every bend there is a red and green signal light. If a guard escorting a prisoner finds a red light in his path he knows that around the corner is a guard with another prisoner. He will push his charge into a wall cell in the way that rail workers in a tunnel edge into a small safety opening when a train is coming. When the green light is showing he double checks that the way is clear by making a special sound—in Lubianka it is a tongue-click—and when this is answered by another guard around the bend he will proceed with his charge. In Polish prisons warders achieve the same result by tapping corridor railings with their keys.

Sometimes the interrogation takes place in an office outside the prison, but the prospect of leaving the gaol, even for a few hours, is not, under these circumstances, attractive. The prisoner is too pre-occupied with his apprehensions. Burney passed through the gates of Fresnes gaol six times but later could recall no detail of its appearance. On the way out he was obsessed with the reasons for his being taken out—it was for interrogation—and on the way in he was too relieved at being brought back alive.

The preliminaries vary greatly. The Cheka confined its prisoners in damp, deep dungeons for weeks at a time, leaving them practically without food and water. There were no beds, tables or chairs;

captives had to lie on a floor compounded of knee-deep mud and blood, and nightly to do battle with the rats. And if even those surroundings failed to affect a prisoner, he was taken downstairs to a lower, wholly dark and bitterly cold cellar. He was then taken upstairs to the interrogators and once more told to confess. If he still proved recalcitrant he was relegated to the cellar for a longer period, and so on until he either died or revealed the "information" required, no matter how improbable that information might be. In other cases victims were awakened by Cheka agents in the small hours of the morning, taken into the courtyard, and subjected to a blank volley in imitation of a real execution.*

Alexander Petrovitsh, Professor of Geography at Moscow University, was in Lubianka Prison from 1941 to 1945 without once being interrogated. By then he could not concentrate on anything for more than five minutes. Other prisoners come out of their secret cells broken, pale and ill, and many panic when they are then thrown into a cell with other men.

Garin, an assistant editor of *Pravda*, was interrogated for four years—from 1937 to 1941. He developed a serious heart condition and twice attempted suicide.

Some men break fairly quickly. Turner, after six months in a cell and a series of interrogations, was ready to mouth in court what his Polish captors demanded. He refers to it as "this betrayal of my faith . . . words of abject shame". His concern to protect a Polish girl whom he loved influenced his judgment, but large numbers of prisoners have been under similar pressure. In comparison with many others Turner's collapse and confession were easily obtained.

Prychodko relates the sufferings of Mikhailo Savchuk, a member of the Ukrainian Academy of Sciences, who was beaten up for sixteen consecutive nights for refusing to admit that a group of his colleagues were members of an illegal nationalist organisation. He told Prychodko he could endure all his torment by imagining that he could see his wife and daughter and by reflecting on their greater hardships than his, and greater still to come for them if he admitted any guilt. But after another three days Savchuk's spirit broke and he stabbed himself with a piece of wire.

General A. Gorbotov, a tough Russian soldier who was a prisoner

* From the *Appeal* issued by the Georgian Social Democrats on July 5, 1923, as reprinted in No. 15 of the *Socialistichesky Vestnik*.

in the Lefortovo in 1938, was so badly treated during one series of questionings that he needed three weeks to recover sufficiently to be questioned again. He endured three such series of interrogation and recuperations. Yet Christopher Lance, under interrogation by an eight-man team of Spanish Republicans, signed his confession after one night's captivity and a single questioning session of six hours. He could have held out much longer, but like many other men he signed the document because he thought this would end the whole tiring business.

Parvilahti, in Lubianka in 1945, was interrogated for twenty-two hours non-stop and after an hour's pause continued for a further eleven hours. After a week of interrogations by night and enforced sleeplessness by day most prisoners will confess to anything just to get some sleep. Begin says that not even the desire to alleviate hunger or thirst is comparable in intensity to that for sleep, after weeks and months of continual interrogation.

After being imprisoned for a time, having no contact with any-body, the captive longs for the first interrogation. He hopes to learn something from a cross-examination, perhaps about the whereabouts of husband or wife, the actions of parents or friends, or the fate of children. No such knowledge necessarily reaches the captive, but he hopes that it might. The more intelligent captives know very well that their examiners will exploit this hope, but they do not allow such knowledge to override their hope.

Another tragedy of interrogation is that, under tremendous pressure, some men and women will begin to mention the names of others. This is one of the great fears of every political prisoner. As the remorseless interrogations proceed, the initial resolutions to be circumspect, to say nothing compromising, not to mention any other name, become impossible to maintain. Authority is not interested in claims of innocence; interrogators assume that the prisoner is guilty, working on the logic of "Well, if you're innocent, why are you here?" The question is rhetorical. Some interrogators work on the principle that each prisoner questioned should yield a crop of ten more prisoners.

If veteran prisoners can get to a new captive before his interroga-tions begin, they give him the basic technique of facing the ordeal. It may be summarised in four points: (1) Never tell anything that your interrogators do not already know. As Parvilahti says, "Once they have got hold of a thread they know all about winding it into a ball."

(2) The best answers are "I don't know", "I don't remember", "I don't understand", "I didn't see". Never say, "I forget", for then the questioners know that there is something *to* forget.

(3) Interrogators always flannel, that is, they pretend to know much more than they really do. Remember this and hold out against being confused.

(4) When you are told to write your life story—and this will happen frequently—make it as short as possible for then it is easier to remember what to say the next time.

However, even this simple advice is not easy to follow under the pressure of intimidation, hunger, sleeplessness, threats and pain.

Softening-up, before or during the interrogation, takes many forms and it may continue for a long time. Lance was affected by his dirtiness as much as by anything else. After months of being unshaven and unwashed he could not face his tormentors with his former confidence. Some men endure more direct agony. During one period of softening-up Kirschen was forced to walk around a cement-floored cell, six feet by nine feet, for four days and nights, with two hours rest every six hours. He suffered severely from colitis and his bare feet were worn to "raw stumps". He had nothing more to tell his persecutors but he realised that unless he invented some story for them they would keep him walking until he dropped dead. Early in his imprisonment Kirschen had endured four weeks' questioning, with only a few hours' rest each day.

Begin had to sit facing a wall, with his knees touching it, for sixty hours; some men endure this for more than one hundred hours. Begin himself thinks that he was fortunate in having to tolerate *only* sixty, but he had what he calls the "self-command" to stand it. A man of disciplined imagination, Begin was able to transport himself into the past and future: his body was facing the wall but his soul was elsewhere. In fact, Begin found his initial interrogations more tolerable than his wartime travels; as he said, during interrogations by the Russians at least he was sitting down.

Every prisoner who has had to stand for a long time in one place and in one position, comes to know the "prisoner's film show". The strain and the exhaustion begin to produce mirages; at first in black and white, then in colour. At first his pictures are simple—

the plain wall begins to crack, peel, disintegrate; then it acts as a screen, with people and animals and things filling up the space disappearing and then returning. Sometimes the images are fearsome, symbols of the captives' tormentors with leering, brutal faces. Others are pleasant escape images of full-blown women, naked, voluptuous and inviting. Up to a point this film show is something of an anaesthetic. But it cannot prevent the inevitable physical collapse.

Ignotus' more brutal interrogations were typical of those endured by many. He was made to stand on his toes, clasp his hands behind him and press a pencil lengthwise between his forehead and the wall. Every time he dropped the pencil, which was frequently, he was beaten with truncheons and fists, and kicked. He lost teeth and his clothes stuck to his wounds. He was forced to do physical jerks, knee-bending to a squat and then standing up straight. He collapsed from the enforced exercise, but eventually managed to sleep standing up.

Yet torture alone has made few men "confess". Sleeplessness, hunger, utter degradation, appalling indignities, threats to families and friends are all more effective than straight torture, especially threats to families. The most stubborn, courageous men have been sapped of all resistance by this technique. More refined interrogators achieve the same result by promising *not* to harm the family. But threats are often carried out; many a prisoner has had to watch wife or fiancée or even his child cruelly treated in front of him.

Non-stop interrogation by relays of questioners is supposed to extract from the prisoner every possible item of intelligence value. The strain produces many contradictions, which the interrogators interpret as proof that the victim has something to hide. Often, in a desperate effort to get some peace and rest, the victim makes up stories in great detail which later he has no chance of remembering. These further contradictions are followed by more questions, so that the routine becomes self perpetuating.

The most fantastic rubbish has been vomited up in the form of "confessions". Throughout the world there must be thousands of tons of paper covered with wholly fabricated pointless and futile confessions, which have achieved nothing but the arrest and torment of quite innocent people incriminated by earlier victims who hoped to make their own lot easier. The situation would be profoundly amusing were it not so profoundly pathetic. Ignotus knows of one poor wretch who was electrified day after day, as he sat in cold water, then wrapped in rag and savagely beaten for not confessing to certain "crimes". He could not possibly have known of these crimes, as they had been invented by another prisoner also under torture.

Another technique of interrogation involves the repetition of only one question; Scholmer was asked two sentences fifty times each, in one interrogation session.

"Were you an agent of the American Secret Service?"

"You admit that you were an agent of the American Secret Service?"

Scholmer, taking the easy way out, made an elaborate "confession" quoting names and places from a novel he remembered. The astonishing thing is that he was able to remember and repeat his concoction.

Popoff was even more rash. He broke down after only a few days of interrogation and wrote a signed declaration dictated to him by a Cheka officer. "I, the undersigned, hereby declare that I have committed no hostile act against the existing regime in Russia, and am quite loyally disposed towards the Soviet power. As a proof of this loyalty, I undertake, should any counter-revolutionary plans against the Soviet Government come to my notice to report them immediately to the State Political Direction (GPU) and in other respects to execute their commissions."

Popoff knew that this was virtually a contract to work for the Cheka but he signed it in the belief that he would be released immediately. It was an extraordinarily naive belief for an experienced journalist. The declaration was only the beginning. One of his interrogators explained that some reason was now needed to explain his arrest, a reason which would not look too sinister. He suggested that a confession of having been an intermediary in the illegal sale of a diamond would lead to Popoff's release. When Popoff signed this confession, the Cheka had him. He had confessed to a criminal and punishable offence, and his earlier declaration made him an agent and a Soviet Russian subject. The interrogators now demanded more confessions which would implicate other people—or Popoff would be arrested for real offences, criminal offences. "I had not expected such an appalling development," Popoff says. "I did not know what answer to make. I saw only that the vision of freedom, which I had thought so near, had now finally disappeared from my eyes . . . Were these people possessed with all the devils, and was it really impossible to talk to them as to human beings?"

The strain of interrogation affects prisoners in different ways. A cell-mate of Mrs. de Beausobre, called Sonia, returned from each session delirious and hysterical. On one occasion, after a long time in the interrogation office, Sonia was half-carried, half-led back to the cell by a warder and one of the doctor's assistants. "She breathes stertorously as asthmatics do and rolls her eyes like a terrified horse. The gaolers and doctors hover about for a while, giving her hypodermic injections, medicines and compresses. Her teeth begin to chatter irrepressibly . . . " They kept her alive. One of Mrs. de Beausobre's interrogators told her, "We only kill those of whom we think very highly and those whom we despise profoundly."

Rupert was reduced to "utter hopelessness and despair" by the continual questioning. At this time, 1947, the Russians were still using bright lights which blinded the prisoner while four or five questioners would work on him at the same time, often asking the same questions as many as fifteen times. But he says that whenever they interrogated him without lights they smiled, "that eternal smile, the Communist smile . . . "

Even a man of Pellico's calmness and philosophy returned to his cell after hours of questioning "so exacerbated, so agitated" that only the memory of his faith and of his parents stopped him from killing himself. During "these days of hell", he gave up praying and admitted to doubting the justice of God. He managed to master himself and went back to his Bible and his God, but for many weeks he suffered from recurring bouts of unbelief and only his exceptional spirit brought him through.

Occasionally, a bold prisoner complains of an interrogator's treatment of him. In 1943 Ekart had a cell-mate, a Moscow lawyer called Serafimov, who was so badly beaten during interrogation that he could not stand upright. He drew up a carefully worded complaint about the methods used and sent it to the relevant official. A few days later he was sent for and examined by a medical committee. These doctors stated that they could find no evidence of maltreatment and Serafimov was given ten days solitary for making false accusations.

It is extremely difficult to behave heroically during an interrogation. At first a man's natural anger, fear and indignation may cause him to react forcefully. It sometimes happens that during a first interrogation, on being brought up from his cell, a confident man will face his interrogators with equanimity, but very few people are capable of sustained dignified resistance. Kim Malthe-Brun, a young German shot by a firing squad on January 13, 1945, claimed to have kept his spirit. In a letter smuggled out of prison he wrote:

The Gestapo is made up of very primitive men who have gained considerable skill in outwitting and intimidating feeble spirits; if you observe them a little more closely during one of their interrogations, you will see them displaying a look of violent dissatisfaction, as if they were obliged to muster all their self-control and as if it were an act of mercy on their part not to shoot you down on the spot for not telling them more. But if you look into their eyes, you see that they are enormously satisfied with anything they have succeeded in squeezing out of their victim. The victim himself realizes only much later that he has allowed himself to be led by the nose.

Now listen, in case you should find yourself some day in the hands of traitors or of the Gestapo, look them—and yourself—straight in the eye.

The only change that has actually taken place consists in the fact that they are now physically your masters. Otherwise they are still the same dregs of humanity that they were before you were captured. Look at them, realize how far beneath you they are, and it will dawn upon you that the utmost that these creatures can achieve is to give you a few bruises and some aching muscles . . .

You come into a room or a corridor and you have to turn your face to the wall. Don't stand there trembling at the thought that perhaps now you must die. If you are afraid of death, then you are not old enough to take part in a fight for freedom, certainly not mature enough. If this obsession has power to frighten you, then you are the ideal subject for an interrogation. Suddenly and without cause they slap you. If you are soft enough, then just the humiliation of such a slap is such a shock that the Gestapo has the upper hand and puts such terror into you that they can have their own way with you. Confront them calmly, showing neither hatred nor contempt because both of these goad their over-sensitive vanity beyond endurance. Regard them as human beings and use their vanity against them.

However, most political prisoners would find such sang-froid impossible. Ignotus says that he felt it would be pointless to act heroically when there was nobody to hear and see him except the men who would beat him to death after his exhibition of courage; he confessed because he wanted to live and because of worry over his relatives. Recalling a Resistance hero in a film who spat in the face of his ruthless Gestapo interrogator, Ignotus says that in reality this could not happen. Many people expected Cardinal Mindszenty to appear in court as a heroic freedom-fighter. His embarrassed, hesitant, apologetic manner came as a profound shock to the public but not to other political prisoners.

At the end of the interrogations it is possible that the captive will be tried, though he is not necessarily present at the trial and may not even know the charge; in any case the trial will be in secret. Only when authority hopes to make political capital, as with Cardinal Mindszenty, is a public trial held.

Even if he is given a light sentence or perhaps acquitted, no political prisoner can be sure that the verdict will be honoured. If the prosecutor is dissatisfied with the sentence, he may simply start over again, often with another charge. He is prepared to dig back half a century to find something he can bring against his victim. So that in reality politicals are in the position of persons whose cases are *sub judice*. At any moment new evidence can be discovered relating to their cases, and this may cause a change in the sentence. It is the job of certain interrogators to go on searching carefully for any fresh fact or allegation which may chain the prisoner to his cell more firmly.

Many political prisoners have tried to find out the meaning of their arrest and sentence. When granted a reply they find that it is usually in the spirit of that given to Admiral Porter and Captain Bainbridge about Philip Nolan's case: "The hearing was secret; no information can therefore be transmitted."

The vicious circle is then complete.

3

The Cell

The prisoner's life rapidly becomes narrowed down to the confines of the cell in which he spends nearly all his time. "No future purgatory in this or any other life will compare with the utter desolation of my feelings during those days of blank despair," Turner said of his early days in a Polish cell. And on the wall of a cell in Helsinki Prison, a prisoner once wrote a pathetic blueprint for captivity:

> Forget what was,
> Don't think of what is to come,
> Take what you are given.

The new prisoner, when first pushed into a cell, does not at first grasp the full significance of what he is being given. Nervous and apprehensive, possibly sore from a beating, his whole being out of its life's context, he is unable to bring his intellect to focus point. His eyes take in the furniture of the cell, such as it is. Probably his first action will be to pull himself up on the window bars in an effort to see whatever can be seen. If the cell has a wash basin and toilet he will try the tap and tentatively play with the chain, which he will not pull for fear that the noise will irritate the guard outside. He realises already that he will have to keep busy and he forms resolutions about study and action. If the cell is clean, with several blankets on the straw mattress, he will say to himself, "Well, it could be worse." If he counts only two blankets he will shiver a little in apprehension. But still the agony of his situation has not reached him. This comes at the moment he realises that there is no door handle on the inside of the cell. The sheer horror of this fact is scored even deeper as his eyes take in the spyhole in the door. The prisoner puts his hands in his pockets in a search for something familiar that will give him security—a pen, a key, a letter. He finds nothing; everything, except possibly his handkerchief, has been taken from him.

Another bad moment occurs a little later. Pellico says, "It is a terrible experience to awaken during a first night in prison." Myrna Blumberg during her first night in prison in Cape Town lay "as though rack-stretched". Waking up at any time is possibly the most depressing moment in a captive's life; it is a reluctant return to awareness of the metallic assault on the ears of large keys unlocking rows and rows of cell doors. The captive wants to sink back into the oblivion and anaesthesia of sleep.

Rupert's first impression of the open air, after eight months in a dark cell, was of the vivid, distinct colours of the country; they affected him so strangely that he had a profound longing to return to "the womb of the cell".

Most prisoners seem to crave at times the known safety of the cell. A man builds up a kind of security behind his cell door, based on a sense of proprietorship for the few, miserable belongings he acquires and his small area of floor space. After a period, whose length may vary considerably, the cell represents stability and he is reluctant to leave it and face unknown and hazardous situations. The cell, in fact, triumphs over his initiative. The captive comes to know his cell as intimately as a monk his rosary. An experienced captive when he feels the blanket of a new cell instantly assesses its warmth; he tries to compute the orientation and elevation of his cell, though this is sometimes difficult. Some prisoners have believed themselves to be in dungeons and years later have discovered their cells to be three floors up. More rarely, the converse applies.

When a captive is, after a long period, moved to a new cell he feels depressed and angry. This is partly because a man who lives with very little in the way of possessions values them highly; to be parted from them fills him with despair, until he develops a sense of proprietorship for his new gear.

The prisoner's attachment to his cell makes the cell search particularly disturbing. The captive's reactions are something akin to those of people who come home to find that their house has been burgled. In 1826, in Spielberg, the authorities decided that prisoners were being treated too leniently and that routine needed to be sharpened. A party of police officials took apart everything in every cell, and made a remarkable haul of petty treasures—writing material, newspapers, unauthorised pieces of cloth and clothing, pictures, carved wooden objects, such as statues and forks, and hundreds of other things—none of them dangerous. Thereafter, strict spot inspections were held, at which each prisoner had to strip naked while his body and his clothing were examined for unlawful objects.

The prisoner's dependence on the security derived from his cell can be used in other ways. Sometimes a prisoner is suddenly moved to a better cell, where he has greater comfort and is given much better food. He is left there for perhaps two weeks and then is told that if he does not co-operate he will be sent back to the dungeons. This happened three times to Edith Bone. The attempts were abortive in her case, but the crude blackmail has worked with many other political prisoners.

It is an interesting intellectual exercise to imagine the details of a cell. Visualise a room ten feet by five feet and perhaps twelve feet high. It has plain grey, rather scruffy walls and one small window, with bars inset in thick glass, too high for a man to reach even standing on a chair. The floor is bare stone, perhaps dry, possibly filmy wet. In this room is a board-bed, hinged against the wall, covered with a blanket or two. Possibly there will be a straw palliasse. There is a chair or stool, a narrow table also hinged to the wall and a lavatory bowl without a lid. The only other items are a mug and plate, generally of tin, and a spoon. There is an unshaded and weak electric bulb too high to reach. The door is solid, has a spyhole and is kept locked. This is a home where a man or woman may live for many years. And, as described here, it is not too bad relatively. At least it has a window and a bed.

Now imagine what this room does *not* have. No mirror, no floor covering, no lampshade, no colour. There is no adornment of any kind, not even something cut from a magazine and stuck on the wall. There is, indeed, no magazine, newspaper, book, writing paper or pencil. No bed sheets or pillow. No towel or toothbrush or soap, no clothes other than those worn by the occupant. There is often not much daylight, let alone sunlight. There is no view except of the four walls. There can be no conversation in this room, no reading, writing, music, playing. After the interrogation period the occupant will probably leave it once a day to wash; he is visited once a day or once a week by a nameless, silent man who will change the lavatory bowl. Once a day a small quantity of food is thrust in. At intervals the spyhole opens and an eye surveys the room. Yet conditions could be worse, for prisons and cells vary greatly.

Dante sat chained to a bench in a dark dungeon for four years. Unable even to lie down or to pace to and fro, he had the strength of mind to survive his ordeal. Bonnivard, in 1530, was chained to a rock pillar in the dungeons of Chillon. Able to walk only a few steps each way he wore a hollow in the solid floor. In one particular small cell in the dungeons a prisoner would spend the night before his execution, though often he did not know he was to die. The gaoler led the captive to the oubliette, a trapdoor, where he was told that he was free and could leave. In semi-darkness he would take a few hesitant steps—and then fall on to spikes from which he would drop into the lake below.

Early in the seventeenth century Geffray Mynshul, an English prisoner, penned *The Character of a Prison*.

A Prison is a grave to bury men alive, and a place wherein a man for half a year's imprisonment may learn more lawe, then he can at *Westminster* for a hundred pound.

It is a *Microcosmos*, a little world of woe, it is a mappe of misery, it is a place that will learne a young man more villany if he be apt to take it on one halfe yeare, then he can learne at twenty dyeing howses, Bowling allyes, Brothel houses, or Ordinaryes, and an old man more policie then if he had bin a Pupil to *Machiavill*.

It is a place that hath more diseases predominant in it, then the pest-house in the plague tyme, and it stinckes more then the Lord Mayors dogge-house or paris-garden in *August*.

Raleigh, in the Tower of London in 1604, would have agreed with him. The Tower was damp and its sanitary conditions vile. The plague began there sooner and lasted longer than in other parts of London because of the filth and the rats. Raleigh reported in 1604 the the tenant of the adjoining room had a running plague-sore and that his own son had been compelled to lie near the woman and her child. But at least Raleigh was permitted to walk on the wall where he was a sort of seventeenth century tourist attraction for thousands of Londoners. The governor allowed Raleigh the freedom of his garden, where Raleigh built himself a little house in which to continue his chemical experiments. His devoted wife lived with him most of the time; her second son was born in a house on Tower Hill, where Raleigh himself was executed.

The turrets at the corners of the square tower built by William the Conqueror were formerly used as cells for the confinement of prisoners of high rank. The Bell Tower, the Bloody Tower, the Flint Tower, the Devereaux Tower, the Lanthorn Tower, the Beauchamp Tower—all held their prisoners. Among them were William Wallace, and Bruce, King of Scotland, Anne Askew, the celebrated martyr, Cranmer and Latimer, Jeremy Taylor and William Penn. In the Beauchamp Tower, Lady Jane Grey and her husband, Guildford Dudley, were confined. Many prisoners left inscriptions on the walls:

> Thomas Miagh, which lieth here alone,
> That faine would from hence be gone.

Yet a famous prisoner lived for eleven years in fairly comfortable conditions. Saint-Mars, chief gaoler for Louis XIV, built a block of cells on the island of Sainte-Marguerite in the Bay of Cannes and here, among others, he entertained the Man in the Iron Mask.* The door of the cell is dungeon-like, but the room itself is lofty, with a vaulted roof, and is well-lit by wide and high windows, protected by cross bars.

On January 8, 1688 Saint-Mars informed Louvois, the War Minister, that he had placed the prisoner, "who is sickly as usual", in one of the new cells. "They are large, fine and light, and as to their quality I do not think there are any stronger or safer in Europe." Saint-Mars was always eager to describe his arrangements for safeguarding the prisoners, and on January 8, 1689 he made an interesting report.

* It is beyond the scope of this book to examine the identity of this prisoner. However, the mystery has been partly resolved. Eustache Dauger de Cavoye, born in 1637, entered Pignerol prison in 1669 and died at the Bastille in 1703. He was masked on the journey to Paris and at the Bastille, and perhaps at Sainte-Marguerite. This man was most probably the "Man in the Iron Mask".

"You command me to tell you the practice, when I am absent or ill, as to the visits made and the precautions taken daily in regard to the prisoners committed to my charge. My two lieutenants serve the meals at the regular hours, just as they have seen me do, and as I still do very often when I am well. The first of my lieutenants, who takes the keys of the prison of my ancient prisoner (the Mask) with whom we commence, opens the three doors and enters the chamber of the prisoner, who politely hands him the plates and dishes, put one on top of another, to give them into the hands of the lieutenant, who has only to go through two doors to hand them to one of my sergeants, who takes them and places them on a table two steps away, where is the second lieutenant, who examines everything that enters and leaves the prison, and sees that there is nothing written on the plate; and after they have given him the utensil, they examine his bed inside and out, and the gratings and windows of his room, and very often the man himself: after having asked him very politely if he wants anything else, they lock the doors and proceed to similar business with the other prisoners."

The linen for the table was changed twice a week, as also were the prisoners' shirts and linen which the prisoners wore, a strict account being kept as they were handed in and taken back.

"In candles there is much to distrust," wrote Saint-Mars. "I have found some which had paper where the wicks ought to be when I broke or used them. I had to send and buy them at Turin, at shops which had not been tampered with. It is very dangerous also to let ribbon pass out of a prisoner's room. He writes on it, as on linen, without anyone being able to see it."

Yet at all times, the Man in the Mask and Louis' other important prisoners were treated with respect. Even the Bastille was not the sinister place that French Republicanism painted it. Franz Funck-Bretano in his book, *Légendes et Archives de la Bastille* (1898), exploded the myth of the royal dungeon filled with forgotten prisoners in dark and noisome cells. It seldom contained more than fifteen to twenty, all of whom were treated with consideration.

Another French prisoner, the Duc de Montpensier, imprisoned in St. Jean in 1793, found himself in a dark cell whose only light came through two ventilators set in walls several feet thick and barred with several rows of iron bars. The cell was so secure that the guards needed six or seven minutes to open the doors. Large iron rings for the chaining of prisoners were set in the walls, but Montpensier never suffered this indignity. Lavatory smells permeated the cell and Montpensier was desperate for fresh air. The Duc thought of his imprisonment as "painful and frightful" but many other political prisoners could claim that, relatively, he was well off. Despite the fervour of republicanism and equality it was realised that a gentleman had certain needs. For instance, Montpensier was permitted to have his servant with him in his cell, although this meant virtual imprisonment for the man. One servant could neither read nor write and after making his master's bed and serving his meals he had nothing whatever to do but eat, drink and sleep.

Until recent times the very famous or the well-born could expect a comfortable if tedious captivity. It is interesting to note the details of Napoleon's "cell" on St. Helena, for cell it was in the sense that he lived in a place of security. Everything was make-shift, the furniture was gaol-like, the carpet scuffed and second-hand, the walls had been patched to hide blemishes and rat-holes, the very small windows covered by plain white cloth. The room, fourteen feet by twelve, and eleven feet high, had a small fireplace with a crude grate and narrow mantelpiece. On this Napoleon kept a marble bust of his son. On the wall hung a portrait of Marie-Louise, five pictures of the young Napoleon (one embroidered by his mother) a miniature of Josephine, Frederick the Great's alarm watch, and a Consular watch decorated with a diamond. There was a plain chest of drawers, a battered plain book case, four cane chairs and an old sofa. It was a crowded little room. Although Napoleon had never campaigned in luxury, he had become accustomed to it at other times, so that it was a great humiliation to be forced into this small room.

Increasing political sophistication and liberalism have not only increased the number of political prisoners, but reduced the probability that a political prisoner will be an important and aristocratic person requiring respect and special treatment. Larger numbers of prisoners are all treated alike in steadily worsening conditions.

This trend was noticeable in Russia in 1884 when, at Byelgorod for instance, prisoners were kept for three to five years in solitary confinement in irons, in small, dark, damp cells. Their ration was bread and water and three times a week, a bowl of soup. They had no beds, no bedding; they slept on the bare floor with some of their clothes under their heads and wrapped in a prisoner's cloak.

In 1908, when Yegor Sazonov* was a prisoner of the Czar, conditions were little better. Sazonov writes:

The only thing which I cannot get used to is the crowd of people and the resulting constant noise . . . Apparently the cell is full to overflowing, but every week it seems able to stretch, as if it were blown up like a rubber ball. Russia never tires of sending us new comrades. Who is not represented here? One meets such excellent people that one is lost in brotherly love for them. Sometimes the very reverse occurs, but that is inevitable among such a lot of people.

Picture our room. It is ten paces wide and thirteen paces long, and not much more than six feet high. There are four large windows. Along the length of all four walls are benches, heaped with bedding. A table takes up the whole length of the room. At mealtimes, or, for that matter, at other times too, the occupants of the room swarm round it like flies. Every fraction of space where the light is better or that is anywhere near the lamp is taken by storm.

The appearance of the cell is quite decent. The walls and ceilings are whitewashed, we keep the floor clean ourselves. On sunny days fresh air and sunshine stream through the windows, and we can see the mountain-tops, in the distance. At such times the place is quite cheerful. Time passes, but it is frittered away, because of the noise that fills the cell all day long. I can only work late in the evening and early in the morning. The others have adapted themselves to working in spite of the noise, but I cannot get used to it.

It might be expected by idealists that conditions would improve

* Sazonov had been exiled in Siberia as an active member of the Social Revolutionary Party. He escaped abroad, but returned to assassinate Plehve, chief minister of Czarist repression in 1904, and the most hated man of his time in Russia. Sazonov's deed was so popular that the government dared not sentence him to death. Condemned to life imprisonment, he poisoned himself in January 1911, in protest against the inhuman treatment of several fellow prisoners at Katorga Prison of Nerchinck.

under the Bolsheviks, but they deteriorated. Melgounov wrote in 1926:

> Certain Bolshevik prisons bear the inscription "Soviet House of Detention". Detention! Why, detention in those establishments is worse than incarceration in the old Czarist penal institutions. For at least the latter maintained no rules against exercise and reading; neither had they iron shutters so masking the windows as to make absolute darkness a permanent condition within them.

Indeed, the cells of the Cheka prison in Gorokhovaya Street, Leningrad, have been described as "wooden coffins", for they were windowless, and measured only seven feet by three and a half feet. Thirteen of the cells held eighty-four captives on a ground space formerly occupied only by three.*

In the Arctic, on Popoff Island in the White Sea, Malsagoff in 1924 lived in a cell-hut about forty yards long and ten yards in breadth. Between 200 and 300 prisoners were quartered in each hut.

"One cannot breathe as night approaches; the stench is awful," Malsagoff wrote. "In the evening, when the prisoners return from work, the huts, full of cracks, holes in the roofs, and draughts from all quarters, are so cold that the inmates shiver like men with fever. It is impossible to sleep at night for the stuffiness and human exhalations. We used to strip naked and pile all our clothes on top of us."

The board-beds were arranged along the walls in two tiers. Everyone tried to get an "upper berth", for a continual shower of lice, remains of food and spittle descended on the man in the lower bunk. An apology for a lamp—a tin containing a wick slightly damped with paraffin—flickered in the middle of each hut. This gave light to the three or four beds nearest to it; all the rest of the hut was in darkness. There was always a crowd under the lamp, trying to read or write to their relations. The absence of light was particularly trying in winter. The headmen of the huts profited by the situation to take bribes for "a place in the lamp-light".

Even these prisoners were in some ways better off than those in the impersonal cell perfected by the Russians in 1930. This cell is generally circular and without a window, though diffused light appears from somewhere. There is no furniture except a bed which is lowered electrically from the wall. Even the washstand and

* See No. 15 of the *Socialistichesky Vestnik*.

lavatory in the cell are operated by remote control. The captive is told by a disembodied voice what he must do and when. When the bed disappears into the wall he must stand or walk about; if he sits on the floor he is punished. In fact, the only time he sees a warder is for punishment.

Solitary confinement, the most publicised type of imprisonment, can have many variations and graduations. Pellico's cell in Venice in the 1820s in part of the old palace of the Doge, had a large window with thick bars and looked out on to the church of San Marco. In summer it was intolerably hot, for it was lead-roofed and faced south into the sun. This torment was aggravated by the thousands of mosquitoes which infested his cell, and bit him into a state of physical exhaustion and mental distraction. He asked to be put into a better cell and, when he was refused, contemplated suicide as the alternative to going mad. Later he was transferred to a cell facing north-west, which was always cold. In winter the cold was icy.

Both cells were better than his accommodation in the Spielberg, a grim fortress prison near Brunn, the capital of Moravia, now part of Czechoslovakia. Pellico's cell in the Spielberg was on the north-west in what had been the fort's ancient moat. It was dark, wet, and an utterly desperate place, as were all the cells here; Pellico called them "dens of wild beasts". Here Pellico slept at first on a bare, hard board despite being in very poor health with a high temperature. He was visited by a reasonable doctor who prescribed treatment, but eight months passed before the prison governor approved the treatment, which included an upstairs cell. The meals stank so foully that Pellico could not eat them and existed on dry bread. He wore standard prison garb, coarse trousers and jacket, a hair shirt and shoes of untanned hide. All prisoners had their ankles linked by a heavy chain, while those who offended against prison regulations were chained to the wall.

Begin, in Russia, spent only seven days in solitary which weakened him considerably, but taught him much. "I learnt from the stifling heat by day and the freezing cold by night, from the filth and the stench of the windowless cage, without any covering, from the chill, dirty cement floor which served as a bed for me and promenade for the rats—from all these things I learnt that there is a worse place than the prison cell, just as I learnt later that there is a worse place even than the solitary confinement cell. Man's imagination did not invent degrees in Paradise. It did create them in Hell. Happiness is indivisible, suffering is graded. When I returned, when I went up to my cell, I was the happiest prisoner in the world."

Scholmer, in the Hohenshonhausen Prison of Eastern Germany in 1949, spent nine days in a punishment cell, a coffin-like room nine feet long, three feet wide and six feet high. But at least he was free to move. Other prisoners were kept in chains in the cell. Scholmer knew of a woman who had spent three weeks naked with her hands tied behind her back, without revealing a name her interrogators were anxious to know.

Malmaison is another Rumanian prison for important prisoners, who are subject to strict conditions and harsh discipline. It is said that more captives have tried to commit suicide at Malmaison than in any other Rumanian gaol; here men are put in cupboard cells, seven feet high and twenty inches square. Food is passed through special holes so that the door need not be opened. Some men stay in this coffin for thirty days.

Rupert, in 1954, had a camp bed in his cell, which though gloomy was centrally heated by a radiator behind an iron screen. He was allowed to read—*Oliver Twist* was one book given to him—and he was allowed daily exercise. He was much better off than Kirschen, who was at one time in a cell which was nothing more than a windowless lavatory whose holes had been sealed.

But relatively few prisoners endure solitary confinement except as punishment for a breach of prison discipline. Overcrowding is the norm in prisons for political captives. Some prisoners seem to prefer to be alone.

Mrs. de Beausobre was one. After nearly three months in solitary she was given a cell-mate, Zoia, and did not like the change. The girl was so intimately and constantly woven into every moment of her physical life that her nearness affected Mrs. de Beausobre's mind and soul. "Her constant presence keeps me down on earth," she wrote. At times she was sure the younger woman was a plant, at other times she felt the utmost compassion for her.

In December, 1950, Edith Bone was put in a deep, dark, wet cell in Tonti Street Prison, Budapest. It was ten feet long and three feet wide. The cell had no ventilation and no natural light; one wall was fungus-covered, while spiders' webs hung from the ceiling. In cold weather the wall next to the bed was glazed with ice, and there was no heating. The cell stank from muck on the floor, yet this elderly woman, suffering from several ailments including arthritis of the spine, endured it all without breaking. Later she was moved to a better cell, in which she spent more than three years, but she still suffered badly from her various ailments and she collapsed more than once.

In Vác Prison near Budapest, in the spring of 1954, Dr. Bone found conditions rather better; her cell was two feet wider, had a wooden floor and was therefore healthier, and there was an exercise yard from which she could see the sky, which she had hardly glimpsed in four years.

However, Vác, where "heavy" politicals were confined, is one of the most infamous prisons of modern times. Here a captive has his head and whole body shaved and is dressed in ill-fitting convict garb and boots. The cells are very small, twelve feet by six feet, and very cold, but up to six men are put in each one. A cell has no furnishings other than the rough palliasses on which the captives sleep, a lavatory bucket with a pervading stench and a pail of water. A bell wakes the prisoners and convict-orderlies make routine rounds to empty the buckets and fill the pails. Later breakfast arrives—ersatz coffee and about one pound of bread per man, the bread ration for the day. Rules change occasionally in gaols like Vác, but generally a prisoner is not permitted the luxury of a daily walk in a courtyard until he had been in his cell for three months.

George Popoff said of his cell in the Lubianka Prison in 1922, "Its dirty walls were covered with a thin whitewash and the only decorations were numerous stains of crushed bugs." He was one of sixteen men in a cell of six square yards. "Like all Bolshevik prisons it was incredibly dirty. Scraps of food, street dirt, bits of paper lay in a thick layer on the floor . . . There were such swarms of bugs, lice and other insects that one could have shovelled them up in one's hands." One wonders how scraps of food could be left on the floor. Later prisoners, such as Parvilahti, would have eaten them.

Parvilahti's first cell in Lubianka was "rather like a cramped telephone box", but Father Ciszek, in Lubianka in 1941, found his cell "more like a hotel room". It was neat and clean, with a shiny wooden floor. His bed had clean sheets and pillow as well as blankets and behind a grill in a corner was a radiator. Rupert, taken to

Lubianka in January, 1954, found the atmosphere "sepulchral" and felt that he had entered some kind of "new twentieth-century Gothic cathedral".

Nazi concentration camps were notorious for overcrowding. In Dachau in 1942, 200 priests were in a room thirty feet by twenty-seven with five priests to three beds. Vrba, at Auschwitz, was one of 400 men forced into a space intended for thirty.

In contrast, Turner in Mokotow Prison, Warsaw, in 1950-51, shared with only one other prisoner a cell thirteen feet by six—"a small, stinking lavatory". It was furnished with a collapsible metal bed hinged to the wall, two straw palliasses and two worn blankets, a small stool with a tiny table, a large enamel basin for washing, and a seatless porcelain lavatory made by Shanks of Newcastle—an ironic touch. He had two enamel mugs and two spoons. In this cell, malodorous and dirty, he spent nearly nine months. Other cells in Mokotow are only three feet wide and sometimes house four prisoners, only one of whom is allowed to sit down. The following year, Turner spent a short time in such a cell.

> We never breathed fresh air into our lungs. In the summer we never felt the warmth of the sun on our faces, or in winter the stimulating tingle of a cold, frosty day. There was nothing to breathe from one day's end to another except the stale, dead atmosphere of the gaol. With dark-rimmed, sunken eyes, waxen faces framed in a stubble of beard, bowed shoulders, hollow chests and shambling gait,we were sorry scarecrows . . . What words can express the utter intimacy of mind and body, when every word, every expression and every movement lays bare the secrets of one's soul? What powers must be exerted to control the vicious lash of a tongue embittered by despair? What restraining hand prevents the fingers tearing at the other's throat in moments of wild abandonment?

Myrna Blumberg was one of nine women in a cell twenty-seven by fifteen feet in Roeland Street Prison, Cape Town. Conditions, comparatively, were good. They had beds, mattresses and pillows, sheets and blankets in the cream-painted cell and they were allowed to keep their belongings under their beds. They had a small yard, in which they exercised and washed. Another privilege was permission to spend up to £20 each—from funds deposited by husband or family—on special needs.

The conditions of cells range from the wholly filthy and verminous to the diabolically clinical. Both are disturbing. Some personalities prefer the filth, which they feel has some honest personality of its own to the cold-blooded menace of the clinically clean. A crowded prison in which hygiene is neglected can only have foul cells. The nocturnal chaos as men struggle through their fellows to reach the urinal can be imagined. Some prisoners sink so deeply into lethargy that they urinate and defecate where they sit or lie. The smell is appalling and in such a cell much depends on finding a sleeping companion of clean habits. In summer heat the stench in a cell holding many people is revolting. Politicals do not rate ventilation or any relief from smells from the lavatory pans, bad food and their own unwashed bodies. In this atmosphere only the physically strong survive and only the very strong in character attempt to revive the men who faint.

However, crowding has its benefits in freezing weather when the close proximity of so many bodies engenders a heat that warms everyone a little. The standard of a prison is relative. Gorbotov found Butirka like a sanatorium, although the cell built for twenty-five held seventy-five, but he had earlier been imprisoned in Lefortovo in Moscow, a sinister place where tortures were applied during interrogations. Most of the "enemies of the people" sentenced to death under Stalin perished here.

When a prisoner has been some weeks in the foul air of a cell he needs support to stand when exposed suddenly to fresh air. Women suffer less than men from this foulness because female political captives nearly always wash their cells so much more thoroughly than the men do. Presumably the housewife in their souls demands that they perform a competent job. Many women, having made their cells immaculately clean, ask for wax, brushes and cloths for polishing the floor. Russian women use a brush or cloth under bare feet and Mrs. de Beausobre relates how one of her cell-mates, who had done some ballet dancing, introduced a new and effective way of propelling the brush with the right foot, which was moved in wide, sweeping semi-circles while skipping backwards on the left foot. She found the movement beautiful and she and the others enjoyed watching it.

Women common law prisoners are generally not as fastidious as women political prisoners, as Mrs. R. M. Youdovicha, a Muscovite

banished to the Northern Dvinsk region during the autumn of
1921, discovered during her journeying from local prison to local
prison.

It was late at night when we reached the transport prison at
Vologda, and the staff met us with obscene abuse before stripping
us of most of our belongings, down to the few spoons and cups
which seemed to us so precious in our desperate, helpless flight.
I felt so indignant that I protested, but of course this proved
useless. And when we were herded to the cells, and I reached the
door of the cell I fairly gasped, for there are no words really
capable of describing the horrors of a place where, in almost
total darkness, 35 or 40 half-dead and half-alive creatures were
crawling about over a mass of filthy, disgusting mud between
walls all plastered over with excretions and other nastinesses . . .
In a cell at Viatka nine collapsible bunks, the bare wood of
which was destitute of mattresses, or pillows, had stretched
upon them some corpse-like female figures. And other such
figures were scattered about the floor—all in mere tatters of
garments. And I scarcely needed to be told that the prison's
cement floors were seldom washed. In fact, never have I spent a
night of horror to equal that first night of mine at Viatka, for, in
addition, the room swarmed with vermin, and constantly my
companions kept moaning and tossing in their sleep, or begging
for water, since the majority of them were sickening for fever.
And sure, enough, when morning arrived seventeen of them
were found to have developed typhus. Yet, when the rest of us
asked that they should be removed to hospital, our petition
proved useless.

If the administration allows it, some prisoners indulge their
artistic and literary tastes in pencil on the walls of their cells, with
work ranging from signatures and greetings to obscene sketches.
However, the most frequent marking is to show the passage of days.
Christopher Burney counted a mere fifty-six such markings made
by the previous inmate of a cell, but an anonymous Ukrainian
counted more than 900 in a Moscow prison. Most prisoners feel an
urge, at least during the early days of their confinement, to keep
some record of time. This is difficult in a cell into which daylight
never penetrates.

One of Pellico's cells had coarse, clumsy coloured drawings on the walls, together with areas of scribblings. Many simply stated the name, birthplace and date of arrest, although some men had written brief biographies. Others, perhaps rashly, had written foul curses against the men who had brought them to the cell. Here and there was a patch of philosophy, such as "I bless this prison because it has made me know the ingratitude of man, my own misery, and the goodness of God." But the imprecations of atheists outnumbered the praise of believers.

One of the wisest and most prophetic cell inscriptions, on the wall of a cell in Lukianiswka Prison, Kiev, reads, "He who was not here will be here yet; he who was here will not forget."

There are various kinds of special-purpose cells. Rosa Luxemburg, writing to a friend in 1917, described a visit from her brother and sister while she was in the Warsaw citadel.

> There they put you in a regular cage consisting of two layers of wire mesh; or rather, a small cage stands freely inside a larger one, and the prisoner only sees the visitor through this double trellis-work. It was just at the end of a six-day hunger strike, and I was so weak that the commanding officer of the fortress had almost to carry me into the visitor's room. I had to hold on with both hands to the wires of the cage, and this must certainly have strengthened the resemblance to a wild beast in the Zoo. The cage was standing in a rather dark corner of the room, and my brother pressed his face against the wires. "Where are you?" he kept on asking, continually wiping away the tears that clouded his glasses.

Some countries, including the Soviet Union, Hungary and Rumania, have a special prison van for moving captives between gaol and interrogation room. The van has ten cubicles, each about the size of a coffin, so that a well-built prisoner feels all four sides of the cubicle against his body. He may have to stand in this dark cell for half a day while being transported. For a man newly sent to prison, the first journey in this van is an appalling experience. He wonders if lethal gas will at any moment be let into his coffin, for he will have heard that the Nazis disposed of some prisoners in this way.

Nobody cares much about transport for politicals. Railway freight cars converted into prison cells are made to hold up to 100 men each, in two layers; the resulting congestion and lack of air is frightful. In Russia men have existed for weeks under these conditions, with one bucket of water daily to each truck—but no mugs to drink from.

Prison trains are so bitterly cold that even young men cannot control their bladders. Rupert found, during his long winter journey from Hungary into the depths of Russia, that his trousers froze to the floor.

Most prisoners introduced to captivity by means of a prison train find the whole process so insane and unreasonable that for a time the absurdity outweighs the horror. Everything happens so bewilderingly that it is difficult to get the new life into focus. This bewilderment can be useful to authority, and prisoners are often moved from cell to cell and from gaol to gaol, just to prevent them from becoming too settled.

Lance saw several grim prisons during his Spanish captivity in 1937 and 1938. In Valencia in 1937 he spent seven weeks in a cell eight feet by five feet; it was devoid of furniture, and the only light came through a small hole at the top of the window. As a "dangerous prisoner" he was allowed out only to visit the lavatory, though once every three days he was permitted to wash under a tap. He existed on lentil soup or rice twice a day and a tin of warm water flavoured with a trickle of condensed milk, though he did manage to supplement this diet with scraps purloined from the garbage heap.

Lance found exercise the only way of staying balanced. He could walk only three paces but in the early days of his imprisonment he covered five miles a day; during his final week he was too feeble to do any exercise and lay in a state of semi-collapse on the floor. Still, he had one advantage not shared by many other captives for he had managed to keep his prayer book.

In November, 1937, Lance was moved from the Valencia gaol to Segorbe Prison, where he shared a cellar with sixty-eight other men, the space allocation per prisoner being six feet by three, which was fairly roomy. Some of the captives were Catholics, others Fascists— all "enemies of the people". Conditions were rather better here, because the prison governor was a more humane man; he sent for Lance to talk personally with him and to give him a few parcels that filtered through.

In April, 1938, Lance was transferred to a crowded, filthy gaol in Barcelona, where he worked at treading sandy clay and straw for brick-making. His bare feet became so bloody that his guards reluctantly transferred him to a workshop.

Lance also suffered the frightful ordeal of imprisonment on the notorious prison-ship *Uruguay* in Barcelona harbour. One of 1,200 captives on board, Lance was put into a padded cell, his only "furniture" a little straw, his only ventilation a small door grille. On his first night on the ship it was hit by bombs during an enemy air raid—a terrifying experience for a man locked up. The harbour was bombed every night. Lance spent a month in this cell, not once leaving it, not once seeing a human face. For a latrine he used a small drain in the corner of the cabin. Twice a day a guard passed a tin of watery soup to him through the grill. Lice-ridden, flea-ridden, bug-ridden, Lance's condition rapidly deteriorated and he became grotesquely misshapen. He held his sanity together only by prayer.

Many other prisoners did not survive; they either died from hunger or torture or were taken ashore to be shot, to make room for new batches of captives. Yet the *Uruguay* was officially classed as a hospital ship. Foreign observers accepted this fiction. Sefton Delmer of the *Daily Express* was permitted to see Lance, who was specially shaved and cleaned up for the interview, so that Delmer did not realise Lance's desperate position. In tones of great reasonableness Lance was told, in front of Delmer, that he merely had to give the names of his "accomplices" and he would be released.

In October, 1938, Lance was moved yet again, this time to a foul prison in Barcelona known as Preventorio C. An important criminal, Lance was taken into a loft and pushed into a wire pen, eight feet by four feet. To his right and left and across a narrow passage were other prisoners in identical pens. Talking was forbidden and each pen was searched twice a day. The diet was just above starvation level. Yet two British consular officials who visited Lance in this gaol reported to his wife that he was not too badly off but was suffering from headaches and dizziness.

Lance's seventh prison, near Gerona in the Pyrenean foothills, was the worst. Cold to the bone, hungry and weak, verminous and ragged, Lance was put into a freezing stone cell eight feet by six feet. Snow was falling and there was no way of being warm. Lance now found, as others have, that in certain circumstances solitary confinement has advantages. Five other captives joined him in his cell. Foul-smelling, beaten into complete subjection, too weak to stand for long, they depressed Lance even more. The six men had to take turns to lie down in the cold cell. Lance's ordeal was made worse by agonising stomach pains.

Prisoners' reactions to cell life vary greatly. Myrna Blumberg, when first put in a cell, experienced a wild throbbing throughout her body and for some reason she could not explain she walked on tip-toe. It is unusual for a captive to achieve any sort of sang-froid within a few hours, yet Miss Blumberg seems to have done so despite her bad first night. It happened from the moment when she decided she was "nothing but a prisoner without thought about anything but coping with life in these high, dark walls". This assessment of her situation brought her some relaxation, although she had been separated from her husband and two and a half-year-old daughter only hours before.

Julius Leber, a Social Democrat M.P. gaoled by the Nazis, wrote shortly before his death, "The loneliness of the cell is by no means oppressively burdensome. I often think of the medieval monks who left the world to give themselves over to their thoughts within the enclosure of four small walls. Many of them found supreme happiness and deepest fulfilment in this. In a book by the old-time mystic, Angelus Silesius, I read this verse:

Men talk so much of time and place, of now and eternity:
But what are time and place and now and eternity?"

Being in a two-man cell nearly always makes people ill-at-ease. Begin had a cell-mate who sulked for days because Begin, the day he was put in the cell, placed his wooden spoon on that part of the table the earlier arrival had chosen for his. Difficulties are specially likely if one prisoner is difficult or if they have clashing temperaments. In any case, no matter how much two men may be in sympathy, they generally end by detesting each other. Each prisoner becomes especially resentful at being "stared at". His reason tells him that his cell-mate is not staring at him and that, under the circumstances, there must be times when he will look in his direction but it is difficult to remain reasonable in captivity.

Most prisoners become cell-walkers. Burney found cell-walking "strangely calming and absorbing". His method was to walk straight up and down, pivoting on the last step in such a way as to keep the rhythm even.

In a beautiful piece of prose-poetry Arturo M. Giovanitti,* gaoled at Salem, Massachusetts, in 1912, described a cell-walker in prison with him. This is an extract:

I hear footsteps over my head all night.

They come and they go. Again they come and they go all night. They come one eternity in four paces and they go one eternity in four paces, and between the coming and the going there is Silence and the Night and Infinite.

For infinite are the nine feet of a prison cell, and endless is the march of him who walks between the yellow brick wall and the red iron gate, thinking things that cannot be chained and cannot be locked, but that wander far away in the sunlit world, each in a wild pilgrimage after a destined gaol . . .

He has measured his space, he has measured it accurately, scrupulously, minutely, as the hangman measures the rope and the gravedigger the coffin—so many feet, so many inches, so many fractions of an inch for each of the four paces.

One—two—three—four. Each step sounds heavy and hollow over my head, and the echo of each step sounds hollow within my head as I count them in suspense and in dread that once, perhaps, in the endless walk, there may be five steps instead of four between the yellow brick wall and the red iron gate . . . nothing is louder, harder, drearier, mightier, more awful than the footsteps I hear over my head all night . . .

* An Italian priest living in the United States he left the Church and took an active part in the Labour Movement. Because of his political activities he was charged with "Constructive Murder".

4

The Structure of Authority

❖❖❖❖❖❖❖❖❖❖❖❖❖❖❖❖❖❖❖❖❖❖❖❖❖❖

Authority in a political prison, from the men who direct that a man is to be imprisoned for political "wrong thinking" to those who implement the direction, has a particular structure. At the very top there is a desire for power that cannot be challenged; in the middle is a need for dedicated and ruthless senior officials of the stamp of Louis XIV's Saint-Mars; lower down are the ordinary gaolers who do the job because they can do nothing else or because they compensate for their own failings by exercising dominance over other men.

Generally, the whole atmosphere of prisons and the degree of severity practised there stems from policy at the top. But it would be wrong to suppose that the man responsible for ordering mass arrest, death and punishment is necessarily cruel in himself. It is clear that Himmler was a sadist, but Dshershinsky, the great executioner of the Bolshevik Revolution, was actuated by the same sense of duty that compels every zealous official to be in his office punctually each morning. He was the most sober, the most untheatrical, the most amiable and the most correct in his deportment of the Soviet leaders of his time. One of his victims, Popoff, calls him "the most honest and disinterested executioner who ever lived, the most perfect embodiment of the type of fanatic, cool and accurate in his calculations . . . "

The policy of individual authoritarians can make a great difference to a prisoner's conditions. Napoleon on St. Helena had had a reasonable captivity until Sir Hudson Lowe became governor in the middle of 1816. Conditions then changed drastically. A petty, spiteful and stubborn man, Lowe saw that nearly everybody on St. Helena hero-worshipped Napoleon, and many of his edicts were aimed at countering this. He knew that Napoleon did not entertain hopes of escape; he could only hope that perhaps public opinion in Europe would move towards sympathy for him. Nothing could be done without Lowe's permission; he decided what the French community could read, he censored their newspapers and their mail, he reduced their living allowances. Napoleon's riding was so restricted he felt it hardly worth riding at all; the children were not allowed to play with him.

The whole atmosphere engendered by Lowe and his assistants was one of petty intrigue, gross discourtesy and absurd suspicion. Bent on humiliating the once-powerful conqueror of Europe, Lowe even confiscated shirts Napoleon had ordered for his personal use and gave them to a relative of his own. The regimentation which followed Lowe's arrival, his tyranny and his oppression broke Napoleon. "Given a routine of life that did not prove a constant irritant, Napoleon might have lived several years longer . . . That he could remain sane, have the power to play, to dictate, to behave normally was in itself a feat worthy of notice and admiration."* However, compared with the conditions endured by other political captives Napoleon lived a reasonably comfortable life.

Nearly every political prisoner learns, early in his captivity, one of the great and sobering truths of political captivity—that it is useless to attempt to interest any prison official in the "justice" of his particular case. For a time the captive believes that among the prison staff there will be somebody humane and compassionate enough to help him, the chaplain, perhaps, or the doctor or one of the senior guards, possibly even the governor himself. The captive seeks interviews with the various officials, pleads his case and sometimes receives a sympathetic hearing. If he is particularly stubborn and bothersome, his listener promises to "do what he can", and later reports that he "took up the matter" with higher authority but was unable to make any impression.

Eventually the prisoner realises that nobody in the establishment will help him. This is not necessarily because everybody in the place

* Mabel Brookes, *St. Helena Story.*

is heartless. Sometimes a chaplain or doctor is sincerely sympathetic, but it is not his place to have doubts about the prisoner's guilt or to be concerned about his innocence. He has been trusted to do his job and to mind his own business. If he were to press for investigation into a prisoner's case he would not keep his job for long; he could even finish up in a cell himself, another "enemy of the state". Also, he is handicapped by knowing nothing about the prisoner other than what the man himself relates. A man tried in secret has no file when he reaches prison. He comes only with instructions as to how he is to be treated. For all that the governor and staff know, the man really is dangerous, guilty perhaps of horrifying crimes. There is no way of knowing. He could arrive at the prison with DANGEROUS stamped on his card, the word is passed around and the captive acquires a reputation. The longer he is in captivity the less chance there is of anybody's taking notice of his protestations of innocence which, in time, become fewer and fewer.

Officials want to believe that their prisoners are dangerous for this makes it easier for them to do their jobs with a good conscience. They are the men who must implement orders such as plans to exterminate thousands of political prisoners. At a great prison camp, like Auschwitz or Buchenwald, there was limited accommodation, even though the limit was sometimes over-stretched by thousands. When the overcrowding reached enormous proportions a "selection" would be made. The naked men were examined in the impersonal way that a manufacturer of clothing weeds out his seconds, and the feeble, the ill and the useless were discarded. It often happened, too, that vacancies had to be created so that a large new intake could be accommodated. Twelve thousand men could easily be examined in an afternoon by a young SS lieutenant. He would accept the card each prisoner gave him, run a practised eye over the naked body and hand the card to a clerk on his right or left—to die, to live, to live to die. If a newcomer to the prison, still strong and healthy, were listed to die, then it was an error. But in this climate an error cannot be challenged.

Stories of the sadism, harshness and inhumanity of guards are countless. One, calling his captives pigs, will kick over their bowls of food and tell them to eat it like pigs; another will spit into the food, or on occasions urinate into it. There are warders who specialise in standing, in their heavy boots, on prisoners' feet, in

67

thrusting broom handles between their legs to trip them, in waking men at night by blowing whistles.

In Janowska a group leader one mid-winter impressed his authority on the captives in a particularly callous way. Little water was available for personal washing, but the group leader carried out what he termed "enforced washing". He ordered eight young men to strip and climb into a freshly filled tank of water. The men froze to death within two hours. In Janowska the Nazis got rid of the weaker men by ordering a batch to remain in the open all night. In winter this meant death from exposure. If any man in the group got up from the ground the guards had orders to shoot to prevent his "escape".*

Madame Spirondova, a political prisoner in the early days of Bolshevism, notes that it was commonplace for governors to specialise in contriving specific humiliations for their prisoners. She saw male prisoners forced to bury executed comrades and women made to wash blood from cell walls after beatings and executions. In Odessa she saw ladies forced to empty lavatories with their bare hands, while men of the bourgeoisie had to sweep gaol yards with silk hats requisitioned for the job.

Of this period Melgounov says:

> Human nerves are fallible, and even Bolshevik executioners can weary of a task for the people's benefit. Hence, in many cases it was by ruffians sunken in intoxication, in the requisite condition of "irresponsibility" for slaughtering their fellows, that massacres were carried out. Frequently I myself, whilst in the Butirka Gaol, could see that its most hardened administrative officials, from the commandant downwards, had indulged in cocaine or some other drug before the functionary whom we called the "Commissary of Death" was due to call at the gaol for his victims, and they would have to be collected from the cells by the officials.

After a time in this atmosphere, every guard becomes dulled and insensitive; it would be illogical to expect otherwise. Some men are hard and rough but not actively cruel, their worst fault being that they make no effort to stop other guards from being brutal and vicious.

It is interesting that several prisoners, notably Bettelheim, say

* Wells.

that politicals usually feel deeper and more violent anger about petty cruelty than about vicious acts. Bettelheim found that in Dachau and Buchenwald "prisoners hated guards who kicked, slapped and swore at them much more than guards who had wounded them seriously". This may be because a slap or kick is a blow against dignity, while a savage attack with a club is a blow against the body; the former has the greater corrosive power, for it makes the captive feel degraded.

In his Barcelona gaol, Lance had to pass a pool of clear water on his way to the lavatory. One night he stopped at the pool, and as his guard did not object, he wet a tiny piece of cloth and rubbed his teeth. An officer caught him doing this and viciously knocked him down, screaming that only dirty Fascists washed their teeth. Of all his experiences, this act and its accompanying insane yelling, affected Lance most deeply.

Even the most intelligent prisoners come to regard their gaolers as superior people. This feeling is based largely on the contrast between the prisoner's helpless situation and the guard's freedom to leave the prison and to exercise complete control over the captives. Koestler, a vigorous, independent-minded and widely experienced man said, "Despite my feelings of self-respect I cannot help looking on warders as superior beings."

Most gaolers act in a superior way, forcing prisoners to treat them with exaggerated respect. The captive must stand to attention in the presence of any official, address him by his rank and speak only when spoken to.

The frequent arbitrary orders and changes of orders which plague political prisoners often result from the gaolers' acute and chronic boredom and contribute to the prisoner's sense of inferiority. On one day the standing order is for captives to stand to attention, in silence and with cap in hand when an official is on hand. The following day the prisoner may be told to keep his face to the wall when in the presence of an official and the day after that he will be expected to say, "All present and correct, no complaints, sir." Orders can vary from block to block within a prison, another source of confusion. But no matter what the circumstances the prisoner is expected to know and obey all orders.

The ordinary guards, the rank and file, are frequently army discards or police rejects. Unimaginative and obedient, they have little ambition, only a shallow comprehension of politics and usually they bear no personal animosity to their prisoners. Senior warders have often come from frustrating desk jobs in semipunitive departments such as taxation. After years of getting nowhere they are eager for authority and power, which explains why so many of them are barbaric in applying both. They are valuable tools of authority for they are jealous and resentful of the personal success enjoyed by many men who become political prisoners, and they can therefore be depended on to be firm. However, none of this pattern necessarily held for SS recruitment; the men in that organisation came from many different fields.

Few prisoners ever see the gaol governor except perhaps at a distance. He is often a dedicated professional prepared to give successive governments exactly what they demand. His professionalism often prevents him from becoming a sadist himself, but he too is vulnerable and can be reported for being "sentimental" or "lacking in spirit". Frequently he is responsible mainly for administration, the effective control of the political prisoners being left in the hands of the political officer, and of the senior warders. Many officials, from governor to guards, themselves become prisoners, while officials and representatives of authority, interrogators and others, who have transgressed the ordinary penal code, are often relegated to being guards. This is disastrous for the prisoners. A prisoner who had survived imprisonment in the Solovetsky Islands wrote in No. 31 of *Revolutsionnaya Rossia*:

Every official in the place, from the highest to the lowest (the commander alone excepted) are Cheka employees who have been convicted of peculation or extortion or assault or some other offence against the ordinary penal code. But, removed from all social and legal control as they are here, these "trusted workers of the State" can do what they like, and hold at their mercy the entire establishment. For the prisoners have no power of complaint—they have, as a matter of fact, no right of complaint, but must walk hungry and naked and barefooted at their guardians' will, and work for fourteen hours out of the twenty-four, and be punished (even for the most trivial offences) with the cudgel or the lash, and thrust into cells known as "stone pockets", and exposed, without food or shelter, to attacks of mosquitoes in the open . . .

A political prisoner becomes acutely sensitive to external stimuli, especially to the vibrations of friendliness or displeasure emanating from his guards. A kind word or gesture can boost his spirits for a few hours, but harshness can depress him for days. Under the circumstances it is not surprising that when a gaoler is humane and reasonable his actions stand out. Koestler was fortunate in finding in Seville in 1937 all but three of the rank and file warders "kindly and humane". Nevertheless, they carried out their orders with the same inflexibility as the warders in the more savage Spanish prisons. Men were executed almost daily, though at Seville they were sometimes given a last minute privilege such as a good meal.

Trenck noticed that when his warders came to him after the first day of his being chained to the cell wall they looked sorrowful and compassionate. However, their pity waned as time went on. This is another regular phenomenon of captivity: after a time the staff take a prisoner for granted. Sympathy gives way to indifference.

Smarczek, superintendent of the Spielberg when Pellico was sent there in 1821, was a decent man who treated his prisoners as human beings, but he was later punished for his leniency. Pellico found at least one warder, "Tremerello", generous and sympathetic. The SS commander of the camp from which Frankl was liberated was much more humane than most and after the war it was found that he had spent much of his own money on medicine for the prisoners. Three Hungarian Jewish prisoners hid him from the Americans until they exacted a promise that the SS commander would be safe; there could be no better testimony to his humane qualities. The senior warder of this camp, himself a prisoner, was more brutal than any of the SS men.

Rupert acknowledges that on occasions the guards in his Russian prison could be human; they would tell the prisoners to stop working and have a rest and would even give the captives a share of their bread and tobacco.

Authority in a prison is not limited to the governor and warders; there are also the trusties, the kapos, the prominents, the nariarchiks. For simplicity I shall call all prisoners with responsibility "kapos", the name by which they were known in Nazi prison camps. In using prisoners to rule other prisoners the SS brought a cruel

71

refinement to political captivity by ensuring that the political prisoners were debased by their own kind. The SS knew that a prisoner given a relatively easy job or made an overseer would drive his charges more savagely than the guards did, so as to keep the guards' good opinion of him. Most prisoners agree that master kapos are as cruel as any guard. A master kapo told Vrba's intake of prisoners into Maidanek, "The slovenly will be beaten . . . those who move will be shot immediately."

The social structure of a prison or prison camp is simply that the privileged oppress the under-privileged, because this way lies survival. The ruthlessness of the kapos was made more profound by the simple psychological fact of unfulfilled hatred rebounding. That is, since a kapo could not express his hatred for his oppressors, he deflected it on to his fellow prisoners.

Sometimes, too, the kapos had more authority and privileges than they had had in civilian life. However, their fanatical loyalty to the authority which had given them this power did not necessarily ensure their survival.

Many kapos are cruel in order to be kind, though the average prisoner cannot be expected to appreciate this. A ruthless kapo is often prepared to sacrifice a few men for the good of the prison block or working party he commands. The last thing he wants is trouble from the guards, so he is strict, for instance, with prisoners who do not make their beds according to regulations; he may even quietly kill a prisoner who offends so persistently that the displeasure of the guards is drawn to the block. If a single man in a working party is not pulling his weight official anger is apt to be directed at the kapo for not keeping his party at full pressure. A strong kapo has immense influence and can easily protect a prisoner he likes; he can even save the man's life, by hiding him or giving him medicine or extra food. A few kapos run great risks and use their opportunities when supervising working parties to steal from rail waggons or food stores.

A minor but dangerous cog in the prison system is the informer, who is possibly trying to win promotion as a kapo. The informers are ready to give information on everything which occurs among prisoners. The more people an informer can report, the better his standing with the warders and especially with the prison political officer or "instructor in re-education". But their long-term gain is small or nil, for the guards, while using them, do not trust them and the informers after a time find themselves on a transport vehicle bound for a tougher prison.

Even prisoner doctors may fall victim to the pressures brought to bear on the kapos. Some are outstanding in their humanitarianism, running great risks and incurring the anger of authority by keeping sick prisoners in "hospital" longer than the officially prescribed period. But others sink to the level of their captors. One such doctor was Maria Nikolaevna, in charge of the hospital on Popoff Island. Highly-trained, Dr. Nikolaevna was a Red Cross worker and had served on nearly every front in World War I and during the Russian civil war. Later she was imprisoned for "talking indiscreetly" about the GPU.*

Her life in the Solovetsky Islands shattered her and she lost all self control. It was said that nobody, even the most disreputable common criminals, cursed with such complete mastery of the art or applied such foul terms of abuse to men and God. Criminals often went to the hospital just to listen to her swearing. No one in the islands drank so much, or drank himself into such a swinish condition, as Maria Nikolaevna. She had reached the lowest pitch of moral disintegration, and human life, for her, ceased to have the slightest value. The hospitals of the Solovetsky Islands were almost a guarantee that the patients who entered them would die. When patients complained of the horrible state of affairs in her hospital, she replied, "The worse the better; all the more of you'll kick the bucket."

Authority may, after a long period, decide to release a prisoner. Sometimes there are obvious reasons, such as a change of government or a period of thaw following the death or downfall of a dictator. Someone, somewhere in the labyrinth of officialdom will mark *Release* against the names of certain prisoners, and eventually, after many months or even years of procrastination, the prisoner will find himself free. In many cases reasons for release remain as mysterious as reasons for arrest.

However, a released prisoner can be sure that, for as long as he remains in the country of his imprisonment, authority will not forget him. Nor will it accord him any rights. Mrs. de Beausobre, released only because she was not expected to survive her various

* See page 79

73

physical disorders, found that nobody would accept responsibility for her. To get a job of any sort she needed a passport, but no official would issue a passport. Without a job she had no money to buy food. It was a desperate vicious circle resolved only, in Mrs. de Beausobre's case, by a chance meeting with old friends who risked their own safety to help her. After a frustrating fight with officialdom, won by bribery, she was rescued by her former English governess, a very elderly woman, and was brought to England.

Other prisoners have wandered for months all over the country, passed from one uninterested official to another until they starve, are again arrested or find somebody to help them. The only real solution is to leave the country, but this is difficult, especially for Russians. It is difficult, too, for a political prisoner to find professional employment; he is an embarrassment and association with him can lead to trouble for his friends and benefactors.

Even the passing of years does not always improve a prisoner's position. Dossiers are never discarded and "evidence" fifty years old is sometimes brought out against a man. The ageing Christopher Lance, thirty years after his political "offences" in Spain, could not obtain permission to visit the country as a tourist.

The psychology of political prisoners is based on a differentiation between the political and the civil criminals. A political prisoner has offended against the whole authority structure, and he must be changed and "re-educated". Many prison techniques are deliberately aimed at forcing the prisoner to lose his dignity, the inner core of his personality, his sense of purpose and propriety.

Kirschen saw the whole routine of his prison, Jilava, as a plan to make the captives "nervous wretches without any will-power". Initially, there is the attempt to damage the personality which is so dependent on little things, such as the hairstyle and clothing. The prisoner is shaved bald and given drab and sometimes comical clothes to wear. He is not allowed shoe laces, for loose, flopping shoes will sap his self confidence. Nothing is permitted that will tend to make the captive an individual; all outward signs of identity are removed. At Buchenwald, for instance, captives wore blue and white striped fatigue dress with a red triangle under which each man's number was stamped. A man's name is the symbol of his individuality, and the anonymity of a number is more demoralising.

In most of the Nazi prisons new prisoners, and sometimes veteran ones, were forced at pistol point to crawl from the front gate to the roll call area without using their hands, to make them realise that from that moment they were no longer men.

The prison system as it concerns politicals is extremely efficient. The anxiety that is built up in them can be enough to keep them in subjection, dogs and guns and searchlights become unnecessary. The captives themselves become instruments of authority, for prisoners, when in the abject circumstances of the Nazis' political captives, sacrifice their own comrades on the altar of their anxiety.

All the SS had to do was establish the rules, such as the one that ordered that the floor of each hut had to be highly polished. No polish was ever provided or used, but the kapos saw to it that the floors were polished. Just as they saw that the shapeless mass of each straw mattress was arranged with its surface as smooth as the floor. The kapos inflicted vicious punishments on prisoners who transgressed.

One of the most demoralising of all prison experiences is the way in which the oppressors look at their victims. Many times in the course of his career as a captive a man will be required to confront his "superiors", from the day he is arrested until the day he leaves the prison or the day he dies. He is at once made to feel inferior in this confrontation. The eyes of the man on the other side of the desk are sneering, cold and humourless. They run over the appearance of the captive, unlaced shoes or wooden clogs, his debility, and especially his apprehension. The interrogator likes to see his victim apprehensive. If a man is apprehensive he is halfway to being amenable. A man accustomed to being treated with respect in the outside world is deeply disturbed when spoken to curtly, roughly and obscenely, and he needs a long time to become adjusted to this treatment. At first he broods over it, because it is so unjust and crude. The captive continually looks for some spark of sympathy, charity or mere understanding in his oppressors and his failure to find these qualities increases his fear and helplessness.

Those prisoners who come into contact with ordinary civilians— this happened frequently in Nazi Germany—have a similar experience. A prisoner is apt to expect ordinary people not connected with prison authority to show him some compassion, perhaps even secretly to pass him some food. But this happens very rarely. The civilian sees the prisoner as an abject, undignified creature; his very appearance suggests that he must be paying for some great crime or sin. The civilian wants to believe that the prisoners deserve their punishment, because then he need not do anything about the situation. He hears that "those terrible men from the prison are unreliable and treacherous, that they steal and are dishonest". They are all these things, of course, but they are effects not causes.

This phenomenon explains why the countless ordinary Germans who came into contact with the millions of pathetic prisoners ignored their existence. After 1945 it was commonplace to hear respectable Germans deny any knowledge of concentration camps. In many cases they were speaking the technical truth because they had been able to put the whole situation out of their minds and memories.

In a similar way the Jekyll and Hyde existence of camp commandants and officers can be explained. At their trials it was repeatedly stated that they were devoted family men as well as being perverted fiends in their prisons. The double life came about easily, for these men had convinced themselves that the beings they supervised were mere inferior and obnoxious, and perhaps even noxious, beasts, undeserving of any human treatment.

In the Nazi camp-prisons the guards forced the prisoners to defile their own most cherished values. For instance, they were forced to accuse their wives of adultery and prostitution, to allege vile actions against themselves and one another, to curse their God. Bettelheim says that this treatment often lasted more than twelve hours. It was not meaningless from the SS's viewpoint. It was intended to break the prisoners' resistance quickly by destroying their own images of themselves—and it succeeded.

A simple way of destroying a man's sense of life-rhythm and balance is to take away his watch. It might be supposed that in prison, where a man has no appointments or specific duties, this would not trouble him. But time is difficult to gauge in prison and a man *must* gauge it in order to plan the eating of his meagre ration. More importantly, if he is one of a working party he needs to know, for sheer survival, the length of time remaining before the next issue of food or before the end of work for the day. He has only so much strength and he must conserve it.

Bettelheim describes the SS officers' attempts to destroy a man's faith in his ability to predict the future. Clearly one of the basic rules of authority is to ensure that no prisoner is able to look ahead to any definite timetable or pattern. Authority may bring in new rules and regulations, unexpectedly grant some petty privilege and suddenly revoke it. A favourite device is to send for a prisoner to tell him that he is about to be released. He is fitted out with clothing—and is then stripped of it and returned to his cell. Another technique is irregular issue of rations. These arbitrary changes emphasise the prisoner's complete lack of control over the most trivial aspects of his life, and reinforce his sense of helplessness.

One of the most diabolical methods of producing this uncertainty about the future is to sentence a captive to death and then put him in solitary confinement, so that each time his door opens he believes they have come to take him to execution. A well-known Hungarian journalist, Sandor Haraszti, endured this for three years.

Melgounov says that in Russia in the 1920s there were thousands of captives over whose heads the Damocles' sword had been so long and so constantly suspended that at last they would even refuse to leave their cells if told that they were going to be released, since the announcement seemed to them merely a trap to induce them to go quietly to execution. In other cases, prisoners who had left their cells in the belief that they were going to be set free, and had smilingly received the congratulations of their fellow prisoners, would, a few days later, be figuring amongst the shot.

Another part of the technique is to move prisoners from cell to cell and prison to prison, so that they cannot become too settled and to prevent the possibility of friendship or sympathy between guards and prisoners. Bettelheim slept in five different prison barracks and worked in twenty different groups; in this way he came into personal contact with 600 prisoners in Dachau and 900 in Buchenwald.

Often the cells are progressively worse, but occasionally a prisoner is put into a "holiday" or "luxury" cell just to make the next retrogressive step all the more demoralising. Paloczi-Horvath was moved from an ordinary basement cell to an even lower one, similar to his previous one except that the floor was three inches deep in water and the wall ran wet. Every morning he and the others in the same section would be given a bucket and some rags to sop up the water, an activity akin to moving a hill of sand from one place to another and then back again.

77

Everything in prison must be done with maximum shock impact. If a prisoner is prepared for any ordeal or incident then prison psychology has failed. To this end guards wear heavy nailed boots which echo and crash in the prison corridors, or they wear cloth shoes so that captives cannot hear them approaching. The silent approach adds to the shock when a guard suddenly throws a cell door open.

The psychology of prison demands that the prisoner be given no information and no reasons. "There is no 'why' here," a German guard replied to Levi when, desperately thirsty, he asked why he could not suck an icicle that had broken off his hut.

Prison officials try to prevent the development of heroes or martyrs in prison, as they try to prevent any sort of individuality. For instance, if one prisoner tries to protect another captive or a group of captives, the "hero" is killed or moved to a tougher prison. The men he had tried to help or protect are also punished, so that the group itself will in future see to it that there are no more heroes.

Ekart, in Russia, made the mistake of speaking for a group of men in his prison camp, assuring the commandant that among this group there were no German sympathisers. This was an error of judgment, for it showed the commandant that Ekart was a leader of an organised group, sure of his men. Ekart was close to release before this incident; after it he remained in captivity for a further five years.

On Popoff Island the political prisoners not only did all the hardest labour, and had to keep their own quarters clean, but were particularly humiliated by being obliged to clean the common criminals' beds of dirt, remains of food, spittle and lice. Whenever a new party of political prisoners arrived they were compelled to clean out the huts, which were so filthy that the task made many of the political prisoners sick. In 1924, it took 1,500 men two months to clean out the camp at Popoff Island.

Ill feeling and suspicion among prisoners is deliberately encouraged. Ignotus says that the best way of making people hostile to one another is to cram them together in a small community. A unified prison community could be a dangerous weapon in the hands of a few good leaders. So everything is done to see that unity does not develop. In any case, politicals are so keyed-up with tensions, angers and resentments that these must be worked off in some way. Since they cannot be directed at authority, they are channelled into internal quarrels. Within the mass of misery and resignation well defined classes develop, especially in large prisons where most prisoners live in communities. Bettelheim, probably the most honest of all observers among prisoners, says frankly (and others support him) that "prisoners could have done much more for one another and the SS would have permitted it, condoned it or been unable to prevent it, if the terrible internecine class warfare among prisoners had not constantly interfered with such efforts".

The whole prison system has the class and status structure of a government department, with each senior passing the buck down the line and each junior trying to cut the throat of the man above him. In the complex machinations that go on continually the captives are caught in the middle and are punished by everybody. Authority knows its psychology is correct when prisoners are seen to give up. Vrba, in Maidanek Prison in 1942, saw all round him men who had abandoned themselves and were nothing more than automatons. This, to political captors, is complete re-education. Whether the man who reaches this stage dies or not is immaterial: he is no longer a threat. Indeed, he is no longer a man. The sense of resignation, of utter hopelessness becomes so profound that men will walk, without protest, to their deaths.

---

* GPU (also known as MVD—Ministerstvo Vnutrenniikh D'el): This is the Russian Ministry of Internal Affairs, the equivalent of the British Home Office. It was formerly called the Narodnii Komissariat Vnutrenniikh D'el or the Narkomvnud'el, from which came the initials NKVD, by which the political force of the U.S.S.R. became notorious. Confusion arises because this force has had several names. In Czarist times it was the Okhrana, in early revolutionary days the Red Guard and later it was the Ch.K or Cheka—short for Chrezviichainaya Komissia or Extraordinary Commission. Some older Russians still call the organisation by the name of Cheka. Finally came the GPU or the OGPU standing respectively for Gosudarstvennoe Politicheskoe Upravlenie or for Ob'edinennoe Gosudarstvennoe Politicheskoe Upravlenie—State Political Department or Central State Police Department. Because of the multiplicity of initials it is often assumed that several police organisations exist; in fact, there is only one.

5

Punishment and Ordeals

○○○○○○○○○○○○○○○○○○○○○○○○○

Apart from the physical and mental torture of interrogations, much other punishment is imposed on political prisoners, some as disciplinary measures, some to satisfy the guards' need for diversion, some merely as a prison routine, according to the theory that regular punishment is beneficial in that it reminds prisoners that they *are* prisoners. Over the centuries man's ingenuity and inventiveness have been severely taxed in efforts to find novel and ever more painful punishments. But modern ones are not necessarily more sophisticated. The centuries-old rack and thumbscrew and iron maiden were more sophisticated than some punishments evolved in modern times.

It must be remembered always that authority sees the captive as sub-human; otherwise the captor would, in many cases, find it intellectually or emotionally difficult to inflict severe physical punishment. Of course, this infliction is compounded with fear and revenge and spite.

It seems clear that most prisoners do become hardened to the pain they themselves suffer and to seeing other captives suffer. The process is probably a sort of auto-hypnosis, a defensive action that enables the brain and body to endure great hardship. Most long-term captives of all periods report that after a time they could witness appalling cruelties and indignities without reaction.

Prisoners can accept even their own punishment, especially physical punishment, without resentment or anger. This is not

80

merely a superficial show of self control; they reach the point where a kicking or beating is completely routine. And by somehow divorcing brain and body they are progressively better able to stand up to beatings.

Threats of punishment are much more frequent than punishment inflicted. The use of threats is often deliberate, as it was with the SS system. Torture and infliction of pain often do not create a feeling of dependency; a man who has endured great pain or suffering without breaking may achieve a high degree of inner satisfaction. Even the man who does break has the satisfaction of knowing that he has lived through a terrible experience. But men continually threatened have no point of reference, no way of resisting or retaliating; this results in a feeling of childlike inadequacy. It is difficult after a time for a man to believe that he is an adult.

"The most painful part of beatings is the insult which they imply," says Frankl, who was deeply humiliated when a guard, without anger, threw a stone at him to bring his attention back to his work—mending a railway track in a snowstorm. It seemed to Frankl the way to attract the attention of a beast rather than a man, and he found the guard's action more wounding than being beaten.

But it is poetic irresponsibility to suggest that insults are worse than physical pain. For some offences in Auschwitz prisoners were sent to the standing bunker, a stone-floored cell about the size of a telephone box without windows. Five bare-footed prisoners were packed in. As only one man could sit down and as survival instincts are strong, after a few days men would fight for the right to sit. It was a dangerous right to win, for the sitting man could easily be deliberately suffocated. This did not necessarily help the others for then the corpse had to be propped up.

Russian punishments, too, are rigorous. "Cold storage"—confinement on short rations in an unheated stone building—is commonplace in Russian penal camps. For many years, at least until 1917, a man could be punished by up to 6,000 whip lashes or could be rivetted to a wheelbarrow for one to three years.

Yet, once in a while, prisoners did rebel. Yegor Sazonov, in February, 1907, was one of many disobedient prisoners taken under heavy guard to the prison office. There were glaring lights, all the prison officials were present, and guards were posted at every door. Orders resounded: "Caps off! Take their caps off! Undress them!

81

Take all their clothes off! Shave them all by force!" The commandant, Borodulin, appeared from a neighbouring room and rapped out his commands one after the other, only to disappear again and hide behind a wall of bayonets. Those who protested were seized; all their clothing was torn from their bodies and their heads shaved. The first two, and in particular Stilmann (a Jewish Social Revolutionary worker) were bashed with clubs. Borodulin kept on shouting, "Club him over the head! I'll teach you to obey! Your very bones will be lost sight of!"

Unusually, all this happened not in secret but before the eyes of a large audience. Towards midnight the prisoners found themselves all together again in one cell. As it was obvious that Borodulin sought for pretexts to punish them and as he could easily find them, the men resolved to make no concessions to the prison regime. They decided not to respond to military commands, nor be addressed in the second person singular, nor to take their caps off.

They lived through those days like condemned men waiting for execution. Every hour, every minute of the day, and all night as they stood on guard, they waited in momentary expectation of the arrival of the executioner. One prisoner met Borodulin in the corridor, did not take off his cap, and was dragged off to the dark cell. The prisoners shouted for Borodulin and threatened to break down the door if he did not come. Borodulin arrived with an escort of soldiers.

"Attention, stand up!" he ordered. The men remained where they were, and explained that they would not stand up. Somebody said, "Return our comrade to us or take us all to the dark cell, because Rybikov is not any more to blame than we." "I take whom I want!" Borodulin said. "Take those two there!" He pointed at two men who were sitting at the outside of the group. The guards tried to seize them, but the prisoners held them and would not let them go. "Club them over the head!" Borodulin bellowed. A fierce struggle began. The men huddled together, held one another's hands and made a closed chain. In animal frenzy, the guards started striking them with their rifle butts. Soon three of the men were laid out on the floor. One had his head split open, a second man's face was covered with blood, a third was groaning and practically unconscious, clasping his breast. The guards had succeeded in dragging one man into the dark cell. Borodulin stood behind them, looking over their shoulders. Something restrained him from continuing the bloodshed at that moment. He ordered the men to be deprived of their bedding, hot meals, and exercise, and the toilet pans to be left unchanged. This rebellion, like all others, gained nothing.

Kirschen tells a dreadful story of the punishment inflicted on a group of sixteen elderly men who had protested during a court hearing that they were starving. Back at the prison, Jilava, they were forced to undress down to vest and pants, in falling snow, and were then driven into a vile, freezing underground cell, deep in water, with more water dripping from the ceiling. Now entirely naked, they were pushed into this cell in the dark, where they were left for forty-eight hours. All vomited and had diarrhoea. Somehow, by clinging together for some warmth and by moving about they managed to survive.

The beatings-up inflicted on captives, often out of spite or sheer sadism, are best left to the imagination. Nearly all those prisoners who have written of their experiences speak vividly of beatings. Some prison authorities carry out deterrent or routine beatings, in which a certain number of men are dragged or ordered from the cells and beaten as examples to the rest. The astonishing thing is that so many survive, although they are badly hurt. In Janowska, Wells frequently saw prisoners beaten unconscious simply because they did not answer their name or number quickly enough at roll call.

Prychodko tells a terrible story of a four-day virtually non-stop beating, punctuated with tortures, in Kiev in 1938. Were there not so much documented evidence of how much a prisoner can endure, any reader would be inclined to say of Prychodko's ordeal, "No man could suffer so much and live."

For many offences against prison discipline—perhaps singing or whistling—a man may be punished by "removal of privileges". His bed is taken away and his food ration is withheld for a day. Most captives seem to retaliate in the same way—by making a noise. The prisoner will hammer his tin mug on the door until all utensils are removed from the cell, and then he will shout loudly; Burney bellowed fragments from Shakespeare. Such protests have no effect other than further punishment, but the prisoner persists anyway.

The most revolting tasks, punitive or routine, are generally allotted to the most senior prisoners, such as high Service officers, or to leading intellectuals, such as professors. Habitually in Communist countries men of seventy and over, already weakened, are made to carry toilet pans for emptying. Senior men are generally punished from the very start with vicious intensity, systematically to degrade and humiliate them so as to make them understand that they are no longer important. The well-bred cultured men, priests, former Service officers and intellectuals suffer most from the periodic beatings practised in various places.

In many prisons warders will charge without provocation into a cell or hut and lash out at anybody within reach. Sometimes they do this when drunk, as if, released from inhibitions, they are finding brutal solace for the indignity of their duties. Wells, in Janowska, was in a hut terrorised for two hours by drunken guards.

Still, it must be said that not all prisoners are beaten or tortured. Menachem Begin, a fair witness despite his lost years at Russian hands, notes that he came into personal contact with hundreds of politicals who were not physically maltreated, though most had been threatened and all had endured mental torture. Edith Bone suffered no physical violence other than one blow in the face from a young officer she irritated, but this was because she was a British subject and not a Hungarian national; repeated efforts by friends in Britain to have her released were abortive, but they had the effect of making the Hungarian authorities careful of the way they handled her.

Mrs. de Beausobre even developed a philosophy for the situation. "It is unpardonable that anyone should be tortured . . . But surely, when you overcome the pain inflicted on you by them, you make their criminal record less villainous? Even more, you bring something new into it—a thing of precious beauty. But when, through weakness, cowardice, lack of balance, lack of serenity, you augment your pain, their crime becomes so much the darker, and it is darkened by you. If you could understand this, your making yourself invulnerable would be not only an act of self-preservation; it would be a kindness to Them . . . "

However, few politicals can create for themselves Mrs. de Beausobre's "thing of precious beauty", especially in the face of all the other ordeals endured in prison. Apart from hunger, sickness is the most common and most varied problem faced by political captives. Authority generally does not recognise the right of a prisoner to have medical treatment; it is regarded as a privilege.

Men of civil, academic or military rank are usually given less medical attention than the others. Kirschen found that the upper class captives were given fewer pills than the lower classes, for the same disorder.

Sometimes, when doctor-prisoners are permitted to give treatment, their fellow captives can expect genuine efforts to relieve their distress, although most doctors are given very little equipment and medicine to work with. Robustness and fitness is not necessarily a safeguard against illness and prisoners with multiple medical conditions often outlive the healthy. Parvilahti and Edith Bone, both chronic invalids, survived while others were dying about them. The death rate varies greatly, depending on the standard of hygiene in a prison, its relative state of overcrowding and the climate. In just one section of the Temnikovsky Prison, in the Mirdva Republic, U.S.S.R., the annual death rate in the late 1940s was nearly 16,000, although the gaol's numerical strength was only 5,750. Ekart, in Kotlas during the winter of 1943-44, says that the death rate in the hospital was 300 to 400 each month. There was no lighting and the medical staff, such as it was, worked in darkness for up to nineteen hours a day.

The death rate among prisoners of the Nazis was also high. Woefully clothed, housed and fed they were exposed to heat, rain and freezing temperatures for up to seventeen hours a day and they were forced to work extremely hard. It seems likely that in many prison camps seven out of ten prisoners died from the cold between October and April. This was the case at Auschwitz. Prisoners of the Nazis had no privacy, were entitled to no medical treatment and could not receive a visitor.

Sick call has always been a travesty in a political prison. In Dachau, for instance, when a man reported sick an SS man carried out the preliminary investigation. He would savagely kick and punch a prisoner and try to drive him away. If the man stayed he was entitled to have his temperature taken. Only a man considered very ill was taken into the hospital. There he had to walk a fine line, for if he stayed too long he could be classed as unfit for further work, and this meant a trip to the gas chamber or to some experimental centre where he would die as a guinea pig. Incredibly, Father Karl Leisner managed to spend four years, with four short breaks, in hospital—a measure of the regard other men had for him.

In winter the Nazis' prisoners could never dry their clothes; nearly all had severe colds and catarrh, which led to more serious respiratory diseases. On a wintry morning, ill-clad, soaked to the skin, and standing sometimes for hours while the roll was called, the prisoners were in a desperately miserable state. Frostbite is common in colder countries for prisoners on outside work are given no special winter clothing. Many speak of being kept standing in snow for hours on end during roll calls. Hunger and cold have odd effects on the ears and many prisoners, after a spell in a freezing cold isolation cell during which they ate practically nothing have found themselves almost deaf.

There can be few prisoners whose lungs have not suffered from prison life; many captives have died of tuberculosis, pleurisy, pneumonia and bronchitis. Few men in gaol for a year or more have escaped rheumatism or sciatica or arthritis, and lack of vitamins and the strain of the dark and half-dark impair the sight. Colitis and diarrhoea are commonplace. Because of the damp and gloom, the lack of sunshine and persistent poor diet, men find that their skin peels and that they bleed easily from a minor cut or graze, which takes a long time to heal. All these specific troubles are added to the general debilitation and weakening. Skin infections, ulcers, boils, dermatitis and rashes are rife.

A captive becomes, after a time, acutely conscious of his body, and what is happening to it. A man who spends most of his time, ill-fed, in a cell, begins to deteriorate physically. From the thighs up, for instance, he becomes thin and scrawny, while his knees and calves swell. Other men shiver uncontrollably, even in summer when their cells are warm.

At one time newspaper revelations about prison conditions imposed on political captives shocked some of the more "sentimental" members of the Bolshevik Party, although they were not able to use enough influence to remedy these conditions. On December 4, 1918 a writer named Diakonov in an article for *Izvestia*, titled *A Cemetery of Still Living Bodies*, described some of the cells attached to Taganka Prison.

These cells, he said, were "choked" with fever patients whose temperatures ranged from 38° to 40°C., and with influenza and typhus sufferers as well. In many cases the sufferers had been ill for a week or more without being removed to hospital. The temperature

86

in the cells was as low as 3°C., but the captives had only a thin blanket or a few wisps of clothing. Diakonov writes:

The doctor who accompanied me around the prison had been in the State prison service for twenty years, and officiated under more than one regime. Amongst other things, he told me that the deaths from insanitation had been very numerous of late, and that daily typhus and influenza were reaping their toll . . . In every corridor, and in every cell, of the "solitary confinement" portion did I see the same filth, the same emaciated countenances, the same hungry and imploring eyes, the same thin hands stretched out to us through the bars. For in that place there were over 1,000 victims moaning, and begging to be released, and crying out that they had been in prison for two or three months without inquiry made, or even for a year . . .

Illnesses vary with prison areas. Tsinga is a disease frequently contracted by prisoners in the north of Russia. The entire body turns into a mass of suppurating sores that ooze pus and blood, and most of the teeth fall out. Since no prisoner is immune from tsinga it is not considered a disease and people suffering from it work as usual.

Parvilahti, while a prisoner in Sibera in 1951, had a dozen serious disorders at the one time. They included dysentery, pernicious anaemia, weak heart, distrophy*, scurvy, pulmonary tuberculosis and high blood pressure. Even his gaolers conceded that he was seriously ill and kept him in hospital for a year; for eight months he was classified "critical" and doctors visited him out of curiosity to see a man who should be dead.

Many prisoners suffer from violent palpitations, brought on by tension, which often develops into hypnotic hysteria in the throes of which the sufferer cannot bend his arms and legs. Myrna Blumberg found her heart "fluttering wildly" every time she heard a distant door scrape open, even though she had no fear of being executed; at that time in South Africa (1960) white political prisoners could exist without the pathological fear that pervaded the lives of their counterparts in Europe.

Mrs. de Beausobre, in the Sarov Woods, ill with kidney, rheumatism and heart disease, endured much torment of various kinds. Even the prison officers who received her were amused to see that

* A slow starvation causing gradual weakening of the body.

she was described on her papers as a terrorist. They were sympathetic enough to see that she was seriously ill and told her to get to hospital as "quick as you can". But she had to work as a gang forewoman for weeks before she obtained permission to report to the prison hospital. It was four miles away and she had to walk through the snow. She was delighted to find that the camp bed had a mattress, two sheets and one blanket—in the Russian winter. She was found to have a temperature of 105 degrees.

In this hospital as a patient, and then as a nurse for a time, Mrs. de Beausobre saw great suffering. "My bloated cardiac peasants are dying slowly of broken hearts. If they are still alive after having done their time, peasants are sent to regions entirely strange to them, never back to their homes. They die because they cannot bear the knowledge that they will not see their own part of Russia again. They love their Damp Mother Earth, but it has got to be the earth that bred them, and Russia is so varied and so vast."

Scurvy is an endemic disease in Siberian prisons. Teeth rot away, gums fester, lips bleed constantly and a man becomes so weak that he cannot stand for more than ten minutes at a time. His muscles start to rot, especially around the joints. Lack of fats leads to "chicken blindness". After twilight a prisoner cannot see anything and has to be led about as if blind. The usual remedy is to boil pine branches in water and to drink the concentrate. Rupert and others cured themselves of symptoms of avitaminosis by eating pine needles.

Begin, in North Russia, saw a young man whose period of "re-education" had been so severe that he had contracted an illness, probably enuresis, which made him unable to control his bladder. He urinated constantly and developed such a foul smell that his fellows despised and shunned him. Most prisoners are afflicted after a time with enuresis and become profoundly ashamed of it.

Captives suffer from prison somnolence and somnambulism. Gaol somnolence is a strange thing; the body feels torpid and half dead, yet all the faculties are painfully alert. Pellico suffered from chronic somnambulism. When he went to bed his thoughts oppressed and depressed him, and he had such acute convulsive spasms that he tried not going to bed at all. He had hallucinations, imagining stifled laughter or groans in his cell, and other "beings" surrounding him.

In Pellico's case it is unlikely that the prison authorities drugged his food to produce this state, but in recent times this has become commonplace. Authority has discovered that chronic indigestion saps a man's will, so they add a violent indigestion-inducement to his food; this, on top of all his other troubles, is apt to bring a captive close to moral collapse. A similar result can be achieved by stimulating a prisoner's pulse rate so that he becomes extremely nervy and irritable.

Surgical operations are carried out under adverse and unclean conditions and the death rate is high. In the Spielberg prison in 1822 Pellico's close friend, Maroncelli, had his leg amputated above the knee after suffering for nearly a year from an agonising tumour. He sat on the side of his bed and leaned against Pellico while the operation was performed, without anaesthetic. The surgeon tied a ligature around the leg and simply cut through it, with knife for flesh and saw for bone. Maroncelli made no sound at all and when it was finished handed the surgeon the only valuable thing he had—a single rose.

In a desperate effort to have a rest in hospital, where conditions are relatively better, or simply to be taken off backbreaking labour, many prisoners abuse their bodies so as to produce symptoms of disease. Some give themselves a subcutaneous injection of petrol, which produces a chronic festering; others break the skin on the leg below the knee and rub dirt into the wound. The nose can be made to bleed by irritating the mucous membrane with a piece of wire. Copious urination, achieved by drinking enormous quantities of liquid, is sometimes effective especially if it is done in association with a fainting fit.

Such subterfuge does not always guarantee respite and a captive can find himself still working. He may reach a state of mind in which mutilation seems preferable to his present existence. This can be achieved in several ways, such as by crushing or tearing a limb in a piece of machinery. Rupert notes that the best method in winter is to put the selected limb on a railway line and urinate on it. This freezes it to the rail in seconds and makes it insensitive to the shock of a train wheel crunching across it.

The mental and physical endurance of prisoners is further worn down by the difficulty of obtaining a good night's sleep. Parvilahti writes,

The bugs were on the move chiefly after bedtime, even though a bright electric light was burning in the cell night and day; the cockroaches, on the other hand, seemed to be at their liveliest in the daytime. Cockroaches do not bite humans, but they came near to snatching the bread out of our hands. If we put our bread ration down on the table, it was completely covered with cockroaches in a few seconds.

At this time Parvilahti's stomach was upset by the poor food and he was trying, despite his hunger, to spin out his ration by eating it in instalments. In order to protect his bread from the cockroaches, he ripped one of the sleeves off his shirt and knotted it at both ends.

The multitude of bugs made a hell of the nights for Parvilahti and other prisoners. When they were taken for a bath and given clean sheets, every ten days, their bodies and their sheets were covered with bloodstains from the bugs.

Scholmer, in prison in East Berlin in 1949, found fleas much worse than bed bugs and lice because it was impossible to plan any systematic campaign against them. He spent May Day that year catching fleas to the music of military bands.

Ekart was troubled by even worse pests—rats. Fat, as big as cats and very aggressive, "their fur and their sharp claws rubbed against our faces . . . they were so numerous it was hopeless trying to fight them."

Kirschen feels that complete adjustment to prison conditions takes about three years. Earlier prisoners have not stated an adjustment period, but their writings in general and accounts of their reactions and behaviour support the idea that three years is the optimum period. "For a long time prisoners had to convince themselves that this was real and not just a nightmare," says Bettelheim. "Some of them were never wholly successful." It is significant that nearly all attempts at suicide take place during the first few months of a prisoner's life, when his depression is most acute.

"Complete adjustment" means the ability to tolerate one's environment, which in turn produces a scheme of survival. The worst ordeals generally occur in the first three years when a man's sensitivity has not been blunted by passive resignation. Moral, intellectual and emotional ordeals are often more damaging then disease and vermin.

In some prisons a captive must ask permission to defecate and urinate, a rule shattering to self respect. The situation becomes even worse when guards delay permission, as SS guards and kapos often did. The captive is often made to report back and give details of his trip to the latrine, another humiliating order. Queues form quickly at the latrines, which are often open, and the strain and shame are heightened even further. In Janowska in 1942 Wells was appalled by the frightful scenes in the lavatories, and in the huts at night when two buckets were provided for many men with dysentery and diarrhoea.

Wells tells a grim story of captives permitted to leave their prison huts to urinate during the night. Before they could relieve themselves the guards made a number of men lie down on the ground for several hours. Then, in turn, each man was made to urinate over the heads of the others, or even to urinate into another man's mouth. This was degradation almost at its worst.

Krishna Nehru Hutheesing, a follower of Gandhi and the younger sister of the late Prime Minister of India, courted official British hostility in the 1920s and 1930s when Gandhi followers found emotional, spiritual and intellectual satisfaction in being put in prison; but there was no physical satisfaction and the other joys soon faded. In the crowded cells Miss Hutheesing found the lack of privacy unendurable; she and her friends gave way to petty irritations and frequently quarrelled. Most of all she missed the vivid colours of nature; she was shocked by the violence, graft and corruption and sickened by the food. "To us," she said, "it seemed the main object of prison was to harass a convict and break his spirits."

A bell sounding the hours in the vicinity of the gaol can be one of the most distressing things in a captive's life. It regularly draws his attention to the slow passing of time; some prisoners have gone out of their minds through being unable to ignore the sound of bells, and through acute nervous tension produced in waiting for the bell to ring. Some men have stated that for as long as they were imprisoned within range of a noisy bell, they had not a single night's sound sleep.

Mrs. de Beausobre says that "No one ever sleeps properly in penal camp or prison. Here the agony in one's heart and mind is dulled during the busy day, but at night it emerges and keeps one awake, wondering, pondering."

Myrna Blumberg, speaking for her companions in Cape Town notes, "We all had the sort of inner restlessness, nagging concern, characteristic, I think, of women in captivity anywhere: men probably find it much easier, if there's nothing else to be done, to forget about everyone's survival but their own; but women, no matter how tough they considered themselves, politically or intellectually, couldn't escape from constant worry about people and events outside, and, from a biological need for family and peace."

But men do not seem to escape from the "constant worry". The letters of male prisoners, their writings after release, their conversations in prison all reflect their concern about people outside. This is especially so in the case of married men; worry about their often destitute families drives them frantic. Some political prisoners become demented on hearing bad news from home, for example that wife and children have been deported to Siberia.

Even for women captives nothing is private, nothing sacred. When women captives are permitted a proper bath, which is rare enough, a female wardress stands and watches them. Mrs. de Beausobre's Mistress of the Baths "would stare heavily, continuously, silently, arms akimbo, teeth slightly bared in a mutely snarling grin". In many gaols brushes and combs are not allowed. Some captives, having sunk to complete hopelessness, do not use them even when they are permitted.

Yet another ordeal is the captive's realisation that he is hated by fellow prisoners and that he hates them in return. The animosity is engendered by the close and continual contact. In Niederschonenfeld Prison, in October, 1920, Ernst Toller experienced this. "Life has grown ugly," he wrote to a friend. "There are only a few of us who want to talk to one another. Do you know that passage in Nansen's book where he describes how his ship lay for months frozen in the ice; and his men bound round their faces cloths with eyeholes, so that they need not look at one another . . . Hatred rages between prisoners . . . "

Even to share the same political opinions does not build a bridge over class differences due to upbringing, differences felt strongly when men are living in enforced intimacy. The man who wanted education but never had it hates the "intellectual". The prisoner who receives more parcels, more money, more books or more of anything is hated; Ernst Toller notes that the hatred was no less if he shared what he had. Political differences also lead to hatred, but Toller saw that the deepest cause of hatred was uncontrolled outbursts of emotion—the prison psychosis.

But later he wrote, "Our internal dissensions have diminished from fatigue, from resignation, from good-nature. I dare not say: from reason—Sectarianism, conceited intolerance, are as strong as ever."

A prisoner may be greatly distressed at the realisation that he is forgetting things connected with life outside the prison. This happens insidiously, as a result of hunger, oppression and introspection; after a long time in prison the average captive probably forgets that he even wants to remember, and his captors' victory is complete. The captive who retains his objectivity learns that variety is not merely the spice of life, but its very essence. Men and women need "the constant ebb and flow of wavelets of sensation, thought, perception, action and emotion". A man preserves his shape, his being, within the context of his variegated existence. In a cell there is no variety and the personality loses its roundness.

One of the most unnerving experiences of a prisoner is to lie awake at night and listen to the guards collecting others from nearby cells for execution. Prisoners develop hypersensitive hearing so that, with a little experience, they know precisely what is happening. No man knows when his turn will come, and as the death patrol's sounds begin, his body and mind grow taut. Is he on the list this night? Toller writes:

It is dreadful to be exposed day after day to the monotonous, constantly repeated noises of this place, where the walls are so thin that from the cells above and both sides and below the sound comes to you. Noise in the corridors, bunches of keys rattling, the doors, with their heavy bars of iron, slamming home, roll calls of names by the warders, shutting of doors, stamping of hob-nailed boots on the stone-tiles or, more dreadful still, the shuffling of rubber-soles. Day after day chains of sound are strangling you with their dissonance.

During the first year I could, by mere will, by a slight effort keep all the noises away and insulate my cell from the sea of noise like an island of calmness. During the second year it was harder: as the psychologists say, one's point of irritability gets lower. During the third year the day came when in helplessness

I felt every noise like the lash of a whip on a wounded head. Every time it cost me a tremendous effort to overcome the many hostile noises and to eliminate them from my consciousness—and that takes a good deal of nervous energy.

In his Auchswitz prison hut Vrba heard disturbing noises, "the moans of the dying and the harsh, frightening, unreal ramblings of the delirious, rising to a shout, sinking to a whisper, calling the names of wives and children and mothers, weaving fantasies . . . "

Popoff was unnerved by other noises:

The treatment of the prisoners by the prison staff was extremely brutal. Many prisoners were constantly accompanied by blows and curses. From the women's cell close to ours came day and night the shrieks of the women and the curses of the warders, who, in their way, were paying court to their female charges. The swearing was almost unbearable. Everybody swore: the warders at each other, the prisoners at each other, and the warders at the prisoners. And what that meant can only be realised by those who know the peculiar objectionableness and obscenity of Russian oaths.

Yet, despite the abuse, cursing and rude behaviour of the prison staff, the prisoners regarded the occasional visits of the warders as the only variety in their torturing, enervating life. Their entrance was always announced by the rattling of the keys. Oh, the rattling of the prison keys! I shall never forget it! Every time we heard it, the question shot through our minds, "Freedom or Death?"—and scarcely daring to breathe, the prisoners awaited the news which the entering warder would bring. For he could utter magical words, although what he had to say sounded very dry and curt.

The prison smell is another evil. No modern gaol for common criminals has this smell; indeed, it would not be tolerated among ordinary prisoners. But political prisoners do not count. Most people are familiar with the smell of people who are merely badly washed; this is only mildly offensive compared with the smell that politicals acquire. Captives are occasionally given a bath or shower, the periodicity depending on the prison. Most prisoners of earlier days do not mention baths; even Dreyfus makes no mention of washing himself all over. Today the usual period for prisoners in groups is about two weeks; those in solitary rarely have a shower.

It is no luxury. Prisoners are herded into the showers and up to ten have to share the one rose, fighting furiously for a fair share of the water before the screamed order to get out. Older, more feeble men often do not attend the shower parade unless forced to do so, being unable to stand the pace or the flying sticks of the warders.

Older men are at a disadvantage in the fight for survival in the group cell. Men mean and envious in ordinary life become vicious in prison. When they see an older man who has obviously held rank and authority, they do their best to bait and goad him. If he has a better bed than theirs they will turn him off it; they will steal his few possessions and jolt his arm when he is taking his water or soup ration. This lack of comradeship disturbs many prisoners profoundly. Protection rackets develop in which stronger and younger men sell security to their seniors. For a share of a man's ration they will undertake to protect him from his bullies, though often the bullies and the protectors are the same men.

Turner says that apart from the "terrible isolation" from the outside world the hardship he found most difficult to support was the lack of reading material; no books, no journals and no paper for any purpose were allowed. "So, once conversational subjects had been exhausted, there was nothing, absolutely nothing, to break the endless tedium of the everlasting days. One had nothing to do except think and think until the mind seemed ready to burst."

The dull interminable routine is demoralising, but a break in this routine is perhaps even more so. The slightest change, especially an agreeable change, heats the captive to an emotional boil; Koestler, visited by the prison barber after nine days in a Seville cell, felt his eyes grow moist and had difficulty in holding himself upright. The barber, a vision from the freer world, was a symbol that life continued. Koestler expresses the captive's reactions to trivia. "Storms in teacups are, for those whose horizon extends no further than the rim of the cup, quite as real as storms at sea."

The slightest occurrence dominates the mind for hours. At one time Christopher Burney was "inspected" by a strict-looking sergeant-major who told him that his hair was too long and that it would be cut. As he left he placed a slab of chocolate on the cell table, and after a few seconds, another slab. Burney was astounded. Unable to think coherently, his brain was a mash of suspicion, fear, delight and bewilderment. He sought frantically for some logic behind this extraordinary gesture—the positive logic of mere generosity, the negative logic of a last gift before execution. Burney intended to make the twenty bars of the two slabs last an entire weekend; he ate them all within half an hour.

Even a change of gaolers is disturbing. Some gaolers, more human than the rest, develop favourites among the prisoners just as prisoners may prefer certain gaolers. The Soviet gaol authorities have been known to change an entire staff of warders four times in four days; Mrs. de Beausobre wrote " . . . we mind it very much; we feel forlorn."

Despite all these hardships, despite the tortures and the punishments and the worries, many prisoners survive. Even despite the hunger they survive. Hunger is the monster of a political prisoner's life. The whole of a captive's being becomes centred on his stomach and all his other desires are sidetracked here, even that of sex. It strikes quickly; within a few days the prisoner is *conscious* of his hunger though several weeks may elapse before he really *experiences* it. People ordinarily eat not only to satisfy body hunger but out of a need for solace. Eating is comforting and it gives a sense of security. When food is provided only in fragments, comfort disappears and a man becomes aware of being closer to death. The stomach may shrink, but there is no becoming accustomed to hunger.

Sanity depends on sleep, but to sleep well a man must have enough food. The overwhelming desire to get enough possesses his whole being and he will humiliate himself to the lowest depths to get just a little more; he will grovel, plead, fight, scheme and steal to get it, for he knows that life hangs by a thread and that if he misses a "meal" he will suffer torment. Most prisoners say that of all the horrors of political captivity hunger is the worst, if only because it is the most prolonged. Bettelheim found in Dachau that "prisoners were obsessed with food and hunger beyond reason". He tells of prisoners picking up crumbs of bread that had fallen into mud, crudely cleaning them and eating them. German scientists had estimated that concentration camp rations would keep a man alive for three months, but they were out in their calculations. Hunger killed many men within weeks, others lasted for years.

Parvilahti, in Temnikovsky Prison, saw prisoners so hungry that a stronger man would snatch the bread out of the hands of a weaker man. "Murder and violent deeds occurred for the sake of a single crust of bread." A friend of Vrba's hid some bread in a pocket of his trousers, which he used as a pillow, but he lost his trousers and his bread. In that society it was accepted that man killed the thief who stole his bread. If the victim was too weak to perform execution he would ask his friends to kill the thief.

Prisoners resort to all kinds of techniques and subterfuges to get the most satisfaction from their meagre ration and to make it larger than it really is. Some prisoners hide pieces of bread around their cell and pretend to forget them, in the way that a man under other circumstances puts away small amounts of money to provide funds for holidays or taxes or expected accounts. A man will hide a crust under a blanket or in his shoe or on the window ledge. Later he will enact an elaborate farce in which he will discover the hidden scraps and will experience genuine pleasure and triumph. Of course, he may weaken earlier and rush frantically to eat the scraps, especially if he hears footsteps that seem bound for his cell. He fears he may be taken away before he can swallow the food.

The captive becomes clinical. Which part of the bread first, the upper brown part or the lower soft part? What to do with the crumbs? Lick them up directly from hand or plate or handkerchief—many prisoners keep their bread in a handkerchief as the safest place—or lick the finger and pick up a crumb at a time and transfer it to the lips? Or perhaps finger-roll all the crumbs into a tiny doughy ball and enjoy the feel of the ball as it rolls around the mouth?

Most worry about what is to be done during the long night when nothing happens. The prisoner is permitted, usually, to lie in or on his bed for only ten hours; if his stomach is achingly empty these ten hours become yet another ordeal of captivity. One way of relieving the torment is to prolong the eating of the daily hunk of bread. One prisoner will break his bread into a certain number of pieces, roll each into a doughy little ball and eat one at regular intervals. Another will eat a small ball every time he wakes, using it as a sleeping pill to restore him to slumber. Another sort of prisoner will keep nothing for the long night, afraid that during darkness he will be dragged from his cell and forced to leave his bread behind. No captive can bear to lose a crumb of food. Most politicals would agree that the stomach is the most secure storage place and that the sooner the food is deposited there the better.

Where a number of men are fed together, soup is served by a

kapo from large cauldrons. It becomes a matter of life or death to be friendly with the kapo; he dips deep into the container for his friends and brings out the ladle full and with a fair amount of meat and vegetables. The others will get perhaps only half a ladle of fluid taken from the top.

Father Ciszek, fascinated by the way various people handled their soup, notes "that some ate it very slowly, using a spoon and savouring every sip. Others drank it down at a gulp . . . Everyone had learned the trick of running his finger around the inside of the tureen . . . swabbing up the last precious drops." Others saved their soup until hot water was issued; then they would water their soup to make it go further.

Many prisoners gulp down their watery soup, quickly wipe around their bowl and rush to join the queue; the ruse rarely works but some men, urged by their hunger, never stop trying for another helping. In a large crowded cell so many men try their luck in this way that they are compelled to decide on places in the false queue.

Rations vary greatly from prison to prison, period to period. Montpensier, a prisoner during the French Revolution, complained that, "Every loaf of bread was cut in four quarters to see if a note had been slipped in, chickens were also cut in two and carefully examined; in fact everything, *even the fruit,** went through this ridiculous ceremony." At times, not having been given a knife, he and his man had to "tear apart the meat with teeth and forks". Sometimes he was able to bribe sergeants of the guard with bottles of wine and ounces of tobacco to allow him to breathe fresh air on a small terrace adjoining the tower in which his cell was situated. For part of his captivity Montpensier and his brother had a private kitchen adjoining their cell and, even more startlingly, a maid.

They were extremely fortunate; rank and birth bring few privileges in the twentieth century. In 1921, at Vologda, Russia, Mrs. Youdovicha and others were served fish in a state of putrefaction, and nothing else, not even the usual gruel, was issued, since the authorities had appropriated all cereals. Vologda was a central prison and exiles passed through it in a continuous stream from every quarter of Russia. The confusion was incredible, and no official made it his business to see what went on in the kitchens, where the utensils were never washed, and the dirt and the food were all cooked

* Author's italics.

together, and worms allowed to choke up the boilers with their foul, greasy, permanently simmering mess of "soup".

At another prison, Viatka, Mrs. Youdovicha was fed a soup consisting of putrid chunks of horse head, scraps of horsehair and hide, some rags, and pieces of a sort of jelly-like substance, all floating about together in a dark-coloured, evil-smelling liquid. With it went some unpeeled potatoes.

Yet upon this horrible concoction the women threw themselves with a perfectly animal avidity, and gulping it down, proceeded to fight even for the potato skins before, within a few minutes, in not a few cases, vomiting. And so the day dragged on, and in time was replaced with the horrors of the night.

Russian prisoners, forced out to work, supplement their diet in summer with ground grass, birch tree buds, berries of various kinds, beetles and flies. A favourite drink is sap from the birch, while Rupert says that in his prison many men smeared industrial grease on their black bread. But at least they *had* bread. Lance ate bread just once in sixteen months, when a compassionate army officer gave him a few sandwiches. In Jilava during Kirschen's time one meal consisted of just over an ounce of maize flour mixed with seven ounces of water per person.

In Siberia, during Prychodko's stay there, prisoners who reached their work quota, whether cutting timber or digging ore, received the standard ration of two pounds of bread and two servings of *balanda*, and sometimes even three or four herrings. It was not much for a very long day of unceasing work in the bitter cold or great heat, of Siberia. But those prisoners who did not reach their quota received proportionately less food, with the inevitable result that their work output fell off even further. In the end, because of hunger, they could not work at all and died. The management was unconcerned about this, for there was no shortage of labour. A cell of 132 men was given a water ration of six gallons each evening in the middle of a Russian summer.

Begin was in a camp where the ration was dependent on the output percentage recorded to the prisoner's credit. In this camp there were four rations, or dixies. A prisoner who did less than thirty per cent of the norm would get the penalty-dixie—200 grams of bread, soup once a day. A prisoner whose percentage reached sixty would get dixie No. 1—400 grams of bread, soup twice a day. Sixty to eighty per cent entitled the prisoner to dixie No. 2—500 grams of bread, and a spoonful of cereals added to the soup; over eighty per cent, 700 grams of bread, better soup with cereals added, sometimes dried potatoes, and occasionally a dry, unsweetened biscuit. Whoever exceeded the quota would get dixie No. 12—up to 900 grams of bread and good soups with all kinds of ingredients.

Parvilahti saw men making porridge out of fine sawdust from under a lathe in the prison carpenter's shop. Many men have eaten casein powder—"cold glue". In Temnikovsky Prison, when the authorities realised this, they mixed the glue with ground glass. Some prisoners beat even this, soaking the mixture so that the glass would sink to the bottom.

Some prisoners, however, report that food is "satisfactory". Ignotus, in Vác Prison in 1950, found it so, "nominally" at any rate. But it amounted only to coffee in the morning, a bowl of soup and another of vegetable for lunch, and vegetable, usually, in the evening. There was a piece of bread every day and sausages on Sundays. But everything was of poor quality and sometimes rotten, and it is difficult to understand how Ignotus could find his rations even "nominally" satisfactory. When working as a translator in prison, Ignotus did occasionally receive extra food, such as tomatoes, sausages and onions.

It is only truthful to say that from time to time, even in Russian prison camps, rations have improved, but such improvements are rare and short-lived. For instance, after Stalin's death in 1953 prisoners were given a little money for their backbreaking work; this enabled them to buy a pound of sugar and some margarine three times a month, plus a small quantity of dried fruit and perhaps even a little poor quality tobacco. Captives of experience report that since 1950 the most efficient but least brutal prisons are in Eastern Germany and Hungary, an opinion influenced by the better food rations given in the gaols of these countries.

One of the political's few weapons against authority is the hunger strike, although it often does not disturb the authorities as much as the prisoner would like to imagine. However, in many cases it forces some sort of action, so that authority will not feel itself an accessory in the damage a prisoner does to himself. Jewish political prisoners, prisoners of the British in Eretz Israel and in Africa, used the weapon effectively. Indians also achieved success with it against the British. But in both cases the weapon became more effective because it influenced public opinion. Where there is no public opinion, the prisoner is taking a great risk. He is, in effect, renouncing his only form of security. Many captives have died during their bravely heroic gesture. However, occasionally others win their point.

In the summer of 1924 some politicals in the Solovetsky Islands declared a hunger strike, demanding that the food should be improved. The hunger strike lasted thirteen days; several people died, and about 100 were taken to hospital. Moscow was appealed to, and this time granted the politicals' demand. From that time onward they began to receive daily two pounds of bread (white and black), one pound of meat, good butter, milk, eggs etc.; these rations were still being issued to them two years' later, only to deteriorate after that.

Sometimes the prison doctor puts in an appearance. He tries to make it as difficult as possible for the captive to stick to his decision. The prisoner is offered tasty, aromatic dishes specially designed to break down fast-resistance, a ruse that often works. The next step is to hint that if the captive persists in his hunger strike he will be artificially fed through an unpleasant tube. A practised prisoner would not react to this hint but the yet-to-be-initiated declares that he will use his last ounce of strength to resist force-feeding. Most prison doctors regard this as a challenge to their authority and have the subject put in a strait-jacket and possibly a padded cell as well. Of course, if a captive is really bent on killing himself he will find a way of doing so; if he cannot starve to death he may refuse water; if he is forced to drink he may try to open his veins. He may even choke himself with a piece of cloth. The most effective counter is to have some sympathetic person tell him that life may well improve, that freedom may only be a night away. "Who knows what is around the corner?" This illusory bribe often succeeds in breaking a hunger strike.

Koestler, in a Seville prison, is one of the very few captives to report that his coffee was worth drinking, but he threw his first issue of coffee and bread down his lavatory. Many a political has done this, feeling that such a protest somehow gives him an active rather than a passive part in the prison proceedings. He soon comes to his senses. However, Koestler had the determination to flush his food down the toilet day after day. This secret fast was part of his plan to convince the prison authorities that he had a weak heart, so that he could leave his cell. He kept it up for ten days. At the time he had a little money and used some of it to buy food; this, too, went down the toilet. He began to eat again only because he was allowed out of his cell for brief periods without having to continue with his deception. Later he drank nothing for seven days and ate nothing for fifteen. I doubt if such an ordeal has been equalled in similar circumstances.

Ignotus went on several hunger strikes for the sake of principle and nearly always won his point. He must have been as lucky as he was brazenly brave, for many others on a similar course have been allowed to starve themselves to death. Through his hunger strikes Ignotus won himself extra food, cigarettes, blankets, books and certain "privileges".

Doctors can be helpful in recommending the granting of privileges and in ordering better food on their own initiative but mostly they are too afraid of authority. In any case, many prison doctors are themselves prisoners without any power. Some doctors, prisoners and staff, take risks for their patients. In Pellico's prison the doctor, when he saw that prisoners' conditions were deteriorating because of the standard gaol food, allotted them hospital diet—a thin soup three times a day, one mouthful of roast lamb and three ounces of white bread. This was less in quantity than normal rations but it was more wholesome. Prisoner-doctors are often in a position to conceal the death of patients for some days, while drawing rations for them; this enables them to give a little extra to those suffering from desperate malnutrition. Hunger is the basic cause of illness and death. *Izvestia* of December 26, 1918, admitted that forty per cent of all prison hospital deaths were due to malnutrition, but the true figure at that time was probably about 75 per cent.

Since there is no hope of satisfying the belly itself prisoners gain vicarious pleasure in talking about food; this is one of the most important activities in prison. Frankl, as a psychiatrist, regards discussions about food as dangerous, on the grounds that it is wrong to "provoke the organism" with impossible stimulus after it has somehow managed to adapt itself to small quantities of very poor food. From time to time most prisoners object to their own compulsive preoccupation and propose other subjects of discussion, but inevitably they return to talking about food and eating. Parvilahti speaks of prisoners becoming obsessed by thoughts of food and talk-

102

ing for hours about how to prepare numerous Lucullan dishes. Miklos Cosmos, in Camp 10, Russia, a noted epicure in normal life, used to entrance his listeners with descriptions of boeuf Strogonoff, Saltinbocha alla Romana, and caviare.

Myrna Blumberg and her comrades speculated about their reunion dinner after release and planned the menu many times. Even men not usually preoccupied with food found their thoughts channelled this way. Leisner, in Sachsenhausen and Dachau, developed an ability to concoct recipes.

Among groups, meals eaten in happier days are a favourite topic of conversation for those men who have been accustomed to dining well in famous restaurants. Meals are described in the finest detail and those of one restaurant compared with those in another. Other men compare the culinary cleverness of their wives. It is a simple form of escapism, though some men weep with emotion at such remembrances.

The most extraordinary feast in prison history was that prepared for Karl Leisner when the young priest was fighting against death from tuberculosis. He sat down to cauliflower, roast veal, roast potatoes, pudding and preserved fruit. In Dachau! Everything he ate had been either stolen or begged, enough for just one meal for one man. The captives who had any part in acquiring and preparing this food must have been remarkably strong-willed to have passed it on. And they must have had great affection for the priest.

Several prisoners who have been able to eat plentifully if not well confess to being sorry about it afterwards. The stomach being satisfied, they begin to think of other disturbing things, such as home. It seems that as long as chronic hunger lasts it acts as a sort of buffer, protecting the consciousness from other hurts.

There can be no other consolation to prison hunger. A man is said to be capable of shrewd thought when his stomach is empty, but it is no aid to concentration. That some captives are able to concentrate shows a clear ascendancy of mind over matter. When a man's memory is his only source of thought and his memory is mainly centred on food, his recollections are apt to be more disturbing than satisfying. In a political prison hunger is not only the greatest punishment inflicted; it is also the greatest humiliation, the greatest affront to dignity.

6

Case Histories

❍❍❍❍❍❍❍❍❍❍❍❍

The case histories which follow have been selected more for their variety than for their fame, although two of the prisoners concerned, Dreyfus and Trenck, are well known for the persecution and torments inflicted on them. But this much the five prisoners have in common: each was the victim, in one way or another, of a political enemy.

Case History No. 1.   Trenck

Many Prussian and German schoolchildren were brought up on the story of Baron Frederic Trenck, known familiarly as "Trenck" in Prussia as a "Churchill" is in England. This is some measure of his prominence, although he achieved little more than managing to stay alive under the most appalling conditions of an eighteenth century Prussian prison. The saga of Trenck is one of the great prison stories of history.

Trenck was one of those men who bring troubles upon themselves. By a mixture of naivety, gullibility and sheer stupidity he was himself responsible for many of the disasters which befell him. His whole life was a series of ups and downs but we can here deal only with his experiences as a political prisoner.

Born at Königsberg on February 16, 1726, Trenck was a member of one of the most ancient families of Prussia. After his troubles he was to write, "I kept no vicious company, was never during the whole course of my life intoxicated; was no gamester, no consumer of time in idleness nor brutal pleasures; but devoted many hundreds of laborious nights to making myself useful to my country; yet I was punished with a severity too cruel, even, for the most worthless or most villainous."

At the suggestion of the king himself, Frederick the Great, Trenck became an army cadet; as a protégé of the king, he remained a cadet for only six weeks before being promoted cornet. At the age of eighteen Cornet Trenck was sent, again by the king personally, to instruct Silesian cavalry in some new manoeuvres. He soon had a wealthy mistress, "who supplied me with more money than I could spend", and for this and other reasons he was content with his life in Berlin. In his first year the king gave him 1,500 dollars, he kept seven horses and four men in livery and he was "valued, distinguished, and beloved by my mistress . . . "

Trenck had a cousin of the same name, an Austrian and at that time an enemy as Prussia and Austria were at war. On February 12, 1744, in Berlin, Trenck was with his C.O., a Colonel Jafchinsky, and two other officers when Jafchinsky asked if the Austrian Trenck was Frederic's kinsman. Indeed he was, said Frederic, so much so that he had recently made Frederic his heir. However, he had not yet acknowledged this stroke of luck. Jafchinsky and the others criticised him for lack of courtesy, and Jafchinsky said, "Write to him. Desire him to lend you some of his fine Hungarian horses for your own use, and give me the letter; I will convey it to him . . . on condition that you give me one of the horses. This correspondence is a family and not a state affair; beside that, I will be answerable for the consequences."

Jafchinsky and the others read the letter, which the colonel despatched. Shortly afterwards Trenck's horses were captured in an action, and the king himself gave him a replacement. A few days later Trenck's horses were returned—from his cousin, commander of the force which had captured them. The king, coldly, asked for the return of the horse he had lent Trenck.

A letter arrived from his cousin, saying in part, "You desire to have some Hungarian horses . . . You must take them, as I took yours from you, in the field of battle. Or should you think fit, come and join one who will receive you with open arms, like his friend and son, and who will procure you every advantage you desire."

105

In short, the Austrian Trenck was inviting the Prussian Trenck to desert, yet Trenck did not destroy the letter but was ill advised enough to show it to his friends and to Jafchinsky, with whom he had recently quarrelled and had nearly fought a pistol duel.

The day after he received this letter, Trenck was arrested at the king's command, cashiered and without any charge or trial was escorted by fifty hussars to the prison fortress of Glatz. For five months he idled in comfort at Glatz, spending freely large sums of money his mistress sent him, although the garrison guards believed it came from Hungary. On occasions Trenck went out hunting, at the invitation of Baron Stillfriede, a garrison officer.

He was, however, in a difficult situation because the governor of Glatz was a General Fouquet, once wounded in a duel with Trenck's father. The Austrian Trenck had captured Fouquet's baggage in 1744, so he had no liking for the name Trenck. Trenck made a hash of an escape attempt, sank to his knees in sticky mud in a moat and stuck there most of the day before the governor gave orders for him to be pulled free.

The attempted escape annoyed the king and Trenck was put in a dungeon. He wrote, "The passions now all assailed me at once, and impetuous, boiling, youthful blood overpowered reason . . . My nights were sleepless, my days miserable. My soul was tortured . . . a consciousness of innocence was a continued stimulus inciting me to end my misfortunes. Youth, inexperienced in woe and disastrous fate, beholds every evil magnified . . . "

He made another wild attempt at escape, wounding several men before being caught. The guards beat him with their musket butts and bayoneted his lip and he had badly sprained a foot. At this time Trenck had only three weeks to serve, but nobody had told him that his term had a definite limit. When it seemed that his attempted escape had lengthened his sentence he tried again—successfully this time—with the help of some sympathetic officers.

From Bohemia Trenck sent the king "indisputable proofs" of his innocence and pleaded for justice, but received no answer. He made his way to Holland, won some money gambling and set off for Riga, intending to join the Russian army.

Of his stay in Moscow Trenck said, "My adventures with women would amply furnish a romance . . . I ought never to have left Russia; this was my great error . . . " But leave it he did, lost a fortune in jewels and money and arrived in Vienna. He led the life of a gentleman until 1754. In March that year his mother died in Danzig and Trenck, going home, allowed himself to be kidnapped by Prussian officers and was taken to the prison at Magdeburg, where he was put into a specially prepared dungeon. For Trenck the moment of trial had arrived.

Trenck worked laboriously and cleverly for six months to tunnel his way out of his cell. While he was working the king visited the notorious Star-Fort and ordered a new cell to be made. He even prescribed the sort of irons that were to be used on Trenck, who heard all this from a guard he had bribed. Before the captive could complete his final plans for an escape he was taken in irons to the Star-Fort. Propaganda was at work in Prussia in 1755 as it was two centuries later; the officials gave out that Trenck was to be executed and later, that he had been executed. This is a favourite ruse of the captor; when his captive is safely lodged in a cell, it eliminates any inquiries after the prisoner.

Few captives can have had the shock Trenck experienced when he entered his new cell. "God in heaven!" he wrote. "What were my feelings when I beheld the whole floor covered with chains, a fire-pan, and two grim men standing with their smith-hammers."

Enormous chains attached to a ring on the wall were fixed to his ankle. The ring was three feet from the floor and allowed Trenck to move about two or three feet to the right and left. The smiths next rivetted another huge iron ring, about six inches wide, around his naked body. A chain fixed to an iron bar hung from the waist ring. The iron bar, two feet long and as thick as a man's arm, had a hand-cuff at either end. Into this contraption Trenck was trussed.

His hands being fixed and kept apart and his feet chained to the wall, Trenck could not put on shirt or stockings in the usual way. The shirt was therefore tied, and changed once a fortnight; the coarse stockings buttoned on the side and a soldier's blue cape was tied around him. On his feet he wore slippers.

Trenck's new cell was eight feet by ten, furnished with a lavatory pan and a very small stool. Opposite the ring to which he was fastened was a semi-circular aperture one foot high, which brought some reflected light through the six feet thick wall. Double iron bars and a grate blocked the narrow half-tunnel.

The dungeon was built in the ditch of the fort; in summer Trenck "could see a mouse run" but in winter it was eternal night. Between the bars and the grating was a glass window, with a small central casement which could be opened to admit air. The prisoner's name was built into the wall in red brick and under the captive's feet was inset a tombstone also with the name TRENCK cut into it and carved with a death's-head.

The double doors of the dungeon were of oak two inches thick; outside these was a sort of foyer, also closed by double doors. The ditch in which the dungeon was built was enclosed on both sides by palisades twelve feet high, and the key to their door was held by the officer of the guard. Frederick had given orders that Trenck was not to be able to communicate with the sentries.

Trenck had power to make only a few motions; he could jump upward a little or could swing his arms in a clumsy fashion; he needed to do both to gain a little body warmth. When he became accustomed to the fetters he was capable of moving from side to side about four feet, although this was painful.

If Trenck's position in his chains was bad, the cell conditions made it worse. Trenck was later told that nobody expected him to live longer than a few weeks. His daily food ration was a pound and a half of bread and a jug of water. Water trickled down from the brick arches and for the first three months he was never dry. He was visited daily at noon, but the visiting officer could not enter for some minutes for the cell's dampness put the candles out and he had to wait for the moisture to evaporate a little. Yet Trenck survived—to endure even worse torment.

The cell was too damp for vermin but a lone mouse came into the cell and Trenck made friends with it. It would play around him, eat from his hand, and come to his whistle; in it Trenck discovered "proofs of intelligence too great easily to gain belief. Were I to write them priests would rail, monks grumble and philosophers would proclaim me a fabulous writer . . . " When the guards took it away Trenck was in a melancholy state.

His comments on this period of his captivity are interesting and significant. "Here I sat, destitute of friends, helplessly wretched, preyed on by all the torture of thought, that continually suggested the most gloomy, the most dreadful of images. My heart was not yet wholly turned to stone, my fortitude was sunken to despondency, my dungeon was the very cave of despair . . . yet was this excess of misery endured. How, then, may hope be wholly eradicated from the heart of man! My fortitude, after some time, began to revive; I glowed with the desire of convincing the world I was capable of suffering what man had never suffered before, perhaps of at last emerging from this load of wretchedness, triumphant over my enemies. So long and ardently did my fancy dwell on this picture that my mind, at length, acquired a heroism, which Socrates himself certainly never possessed . . . "

After eleven months of captivity Trenck's ration was increased; he was to be allowed as much bread as he could eat. On the first occasion, this man who had been a gourmet, shed "tears of pleasure" at being provided with enough bread to fill his belly. But pleasure was short-lived. His restricted diet had weakened his digestive system. With the excess bread and accompanying long draughts of water he suffered from cramp, swelling and gastric pains. He suffered more this night than on any other and when the guards came next day they found the captive in a pitiable condition. They left him some more bread and water, shrugged their shoulders and left him. Trenck could not eat for a further three days and began to consider suicide "for a thousand reasons". Patience, he decided was absurd; release was so distant as not even to be hoped for. He planned to wait a further week and then, on July 4, to jump on to the bayonets of the guards.

Many a captive has "waited another week". In this week Trenck, using a knife he had secreted, managed with many injuries to himself to free himself of his chains. He worked on, always in darkness, cutting through the doors. But before his guards came he had to replace the chains. Forcing his hands through the cufflinks was so agonising that sometimes he had to defer his labours until his hands and wrists lost their swelling. While he worked sweat flowed from his body, his fingers were clotted with blood and his lacerated hands were one continuous wound.

He was making good progress when his knife broke. Crazy with frustration, Trenck seized the broken knife, gashed the veins of his left arm and foot, sat down tranquilly and watched the blood flow. Then he had to strip his shirt and bind the wounds. Trenck lay half dead for days, unironed and in peace; he was even given broth. He suffered from severe pains in most parts of his body and longed to see the sun. Then the officials put him back in irons, though the main chain which fastened him to the wall was thicker than before. Also they deprived him of his bed.

"When I contemplated . . . my former splendour in Berlin and Moscow and compared it with the dreadful reverse I was sunk in grief or roused to indignation," he wrote. "Pride, the justness of my cause, the unbounded confidence I had in my own resolution and the labours of an inventive head and iron body these only could have preserved my life."

Yet Trenck slept soundly and felt sorry for generals and others that they could not sleep with as quiet a conscience as he. He made himself tired by swinging his arms, bending the upper part of his body about and jumping upward.

"Often did I reflect," he writes, "how much happier I was than those tortured on the bed of sickness, by gout, stone and other diseases terrible to man. How much happier was I in innocence than the malefactor doomed to suffer the pangs of death, the ignominy of men and the horrors of internal guilt."

He became more accustomed to his irons, so that he could comb out his long hair with one hand, his beard, long unshaven, he plucked out gradually by the root. The pain at first was great, especially around the lips, but he performed this once every six weeks or two months.

Love was a prime reason for living. He had left behind in Vienna a "lady for whom the world was still dear" to him, whom he would "neither desert nor afflict". He had other strengths, too. "I had read much and loved it, and seen much of the world; vacuity of thought therefore I was little troubled with. The former transactions of my life, what had happened, and the remembrance of the persons I had known, I resolved so often in my mind that they became as familiar and connected as if the events had been each written in the order they occurred. Habit made this mental exercise so perfect to me that I could compose speeches, fables, odes, satires all of which I repeated aloud and had so stored my memory with them that I was enabled, after I had obtained my freedom, to commit to writing two volumes of these my prison labours."

Having no bed now, Trenck had to sit on the bare ground and lean his head against the damp wall. The chains that descended from the neck collar he had to support first with one hand, then with the other. Had he thrown them behind they would have strangled him;

110

when hanging forward they gave him violent headaches. Lack of sound sleep was too damaging and this iron man fell ill with a fever. The governor, Borck, would do nothing to help him. Years later this angered Trenck more than most aspects of his imprisonment.

"Reason, fortitude, heroism, all the noble qualities of the mind decay when the corporal faculties are diseased and the remembrance of my sufferings at this dreadful moment still agitates, still inflames my blood, so as almost to prevent an attempt to describe what they were."

He was ill for more than two months and had scarcely strength to lift the water jug to his mouth. He had a high temperature, violent headaches, inflamed and aching joints and limbs. Once, when he dropped his jug, he was twenty-four hours without water, so that next day the inspecting party supposed he had died at last.

When Trenck recovered from this desperate illness the order came from above—whether from the king or from Borck is not known—that Trenck was to be prevented from sleeping. The guards were ordered to call Trenck every fifteen minutes. Trenck found this torture "unexampled in the history even of tyranny". One of his few friends, a major, advised him not to answer the guard's call, which produced a compromise. The governor restored Trenck's bed and Trenck promised to answer the guard's shout.

Trenck did not then know it, but his case was a subject of gossip in Magdeburg and influential ladies had been pressing for some alleviation of the prisoner's sufferings and for, at least, the restoration of his bed. Through the help of the sympathetic guard and a few officers Trenck was able to bribe—the grenadier guard had been able to make contact with a friend of Trenck in Vienna and get money—he could again divest himself of his chains; sometimes he even had a sausage to eat.

Again Trenck burrowed towards freedom, a long exhausting job. Three feet from freedom he was discovered and re-ironed more severely than before; once more he lost his bed, leading to a second bout of fever.

At times he reached such a state of resignation that he could write later, "I passed eighteen months calmly and without further attempt" (at escape). Yet, in the years he stayed in Star-Fort, he did make two

111

other protracted attempts to get out; in one he was buried under a fall of earth and spent eight hours freeing himself.

If he escaped, Trenck planned to throw himself on King Frederick's mercy, an idea which Trenck saw years later as "extravagant, absurd, pitiable, stupid". Trenck was so incredibly naive as to propose a bargain. He told the deputy governor and other officers that he could escape when he chose; would they ask Prince Ferdinand of Magdeburg if he would intercede with the king should Trenck "prove" his innocence by appearing before the prince, despite all obstacles. The deputy governor pledged his word that if Trenck would show him his method of escape he would reveal it to nobody and would do as he asked. And Trenck believed him! He took off his chains, showed the officers his complex escape mechanism, his keys, his money, pistols—everything.

Thereupon Trenck was moved from his cell while another and stronger one was built. As an experienced prisoner, Trenck should have known that there is no honour among gaolers of political prisoners, that they are not "officers and gentlemen" in the Service fashion. All his work had gone for nothing and he was now in a cell that was tunnel proof; again he was chained to a wall, with a chain of more efficient links. Trenck still wrote poems, but they were despondent now, for even his incurable optimism was deteriorating. But in the end, ten years after his incarceration, Trenck was freed on the intercession of the Prince of Magdeburg.

For some weeks after he was freed Trenck was absentminded and generally deep in thought—"The objects of sight appeared but as the divisions of sleep." He often stopped in the street to stare about him; he doubted his own existence and sometimes bit his finger to convince himself that he was alive. If he was in the company of many people their "prattle" distracted his mind, and the lights so overcame his eyes that he would return home with a headache, lassitude and melancholy.

Trenck was a prisoner of royal whim, agitated by the jealousy of a comrade. Nothing that Trenck said or did could have aided his country's enemies, even had he wished to aid them. The omnipotent Frederick had no reason to imprison the young Trenck, a man devoted to him. Perhaps he was punished to encourage the others to show greater zeal and to obviate the risk of any officer helping the Austrian enemy. This could explain his first imprisonment. His later, more diabolical sentence to solitary confinement while chained to a wall was the result of royal spleen, for Frederick was irritated at Trenck's escape.

Trenck was yet another example of the dangers of living under a despot, who can dispense "justice" without the conventional preliminary of a trial or court martial. It might be supposed that Trenck's ordeal would turn his mind. But his memoirs betray no aberration or lack of coherence—only bitterness.

Case History No. 2. Nolan

Philip Nolan was brought up on a plantation in Mississippi and apparently worked as a cattle hand in Texas before joining the army in Mississippi about the year 1800; some details of his life are difficult to verify because his records were among those destroyed in August, 1814, when General Robert Ross and his British army sacked and burnt Washington during the American-English war of that year.

Nolan's ability won him rapid promotion to lieutenant and one contemporary described him as "as fine a young officer as there was in the 'Legion of the West' ". Ambitious, Nolan interested himself in politics and soon met and was influenced by Aaron Burr, a gifted but unlucky politician and lawyer. In 1804 Burr was a candidate for President of the United States but was beaten by Alexander Hamilton, Secretary of the Treasury. Hamilton made unpleasant accusations about Burr's character, so in the manner of the day Burr challenged his enemy to a duel and shot him dead.

Charged with murder, Burr fled to Louisiana where he owned a large area of territory. The United States had only recently acquired Louisiana from France as part of the famous "Louisiana purchase". Burr, an impractical idealist, set about attracting settlers to what he planned as a new, utopian state. More than this, he intended to raise an army to seize Mexico for the United States in the event of a war with Spain, which at that time seemed likely. His younger friend, Philip Nolan, was to be one of the leaders of this force. Burr's motives were probably mixed; some people said that he intended to make himself "king" of the territory he owned already and of that he planned to capture, but his friends claimed that he merely intended to colonise the region for the United States. His political enemies had him charged with treason, but after a sensational trial in Richmond, Virginia, he was acquitted.

Several of his supporters, including Nolan, were also charged. Nolan appeared before a court martial at Fort Adams on September 23, 1807, where he protested that he had always been loyal to his country. Exasperated and frustrated, anticipating the ruin of his military career, Nolan was not nearly as cool as his friend Burr. The court asked him for evidence that he had always been a loyal subject of the United States. Impatient at the delays and repetitions, Nolan shouted, "Damn the United States! I wish I may never hear of the United States again!"

There was no uproar at this, only a dead, flat silence. The court president, Colonel Morgan, an elderly and conservative officer, is said to have blanched and shaken. He adjourned the court to consider its verdict, which many observers, including Nolan, expected to be a long gaol sentence at least and death at the most.

Colonel Morgan returned to an expectant courtroom and announced the verdict: "The court decides, subject to the approval of the President, that you never hear the name of the United States again." This was such an anti-climax that Nolan laughed heartily; even spectators were amused by this unorthodox sentence. But it was no joke. Colonel Morgan set off to see the President, Thomas Jefferson. Nolan was sent under escort to New Orleans, where he was taken aboard the U.S.S. *Nautilus*, which put to sea. Before the ship returned Jefferson approved the court's sentence and the details were settled: Nolan was never again to set foot on American soil and was never to hear any word spoken or to read about his native land.

The exquisite refinement of this sentence probably took a little time to penetrate into Nolan's mind. He probably believed that a sentence of this type would be impossible to enforce and that, in any case, after a few years it would be revoked. But he learnt that a political detainee can expect no mercy.

Nolan was transferred directly from the *Nautilus* to another ship setting off on a long cruise. The secretary of the navy sent the captain detailed written instructions which he was enjoined to carry out with "meticulous care" and to pass on to any other captain who might become Nolan's gaoler. Nolan was to be provided with "such quarters, rations and clothing as would be proper for an officer of his late rank if he were a passenger on your vessel on the business of his government". The instructions insisted that Nolan was never to be unnecessarily reminded that he was a prisoner, "but under no circumstances is he ever to hear of his country or to see any information regarding it". The document's concluding sentence was, "It is the intention of this Government that he shall never again see the country which he has disowned."

Nolan found at first that his sentence was not too oppressive. Ships' officers treated him with courtesy and there was something attractive about the novelty of his situation. Many politicals have experienced the same initial reaction, even in less attractive prisons than a man-o'-war. Nolan had plenty to read, though all books and magazines—he was allowed no American newspapers—were thoroughly censored before he received them. Any paragraphs, pictures or advertisements referring to the United States were cut out.

It did not take this sensitive man long to realise that while the officers treated him well, he was not a welcome guest in a mess. The most common topic of conversation among a group of ships' officers was home; Nolan's presence eliminated any chance of talking about it. He spent more time in his own quarters, which were comfortably appointed, and even had most of his meals there, his only companion being his servant. He was entitled to entertain officers but he rarely did so after the first year. Strong willed, he was able to wear a mask little more revealing than that of Louis' prisoner in France. The mask concealed considerable emotion and anguish, for after a time Nolan realised that this was no fantastic game he was playing; he was in perpetual penance. But on a few occasions he broke down. When one ship on which he was imprisoned called at Cape Town, probably in 1810, the captain borrowed some books from an English naval surgeon. One was Scott's recently published "Lay of the Last Minstrel". The American officers had not seen the verses before and as so many wanted to read them and time was short before they had to be returned members of the mess took turns at reading aloud the stirring patriotic verses. Nolan's turn came and he began to read the stanza that was to become familiar throughout the English-speaking world:

> Breathes there a man with soul so dead,
> Who never to himself hath said:
> "This is my own, my native land!"

The atmosphere in the mess grew strained, for Nolan's voice faltered and as he read on his body seemed to become contorted:

> Whose heart hath never within him burned,
> As home his footsteps he hath turned
> From wandering on a foreign strand?

Few of the officers present could have experienced a more embarrassing, emotional moment; possibly no captive ever had so many witnesses to the misery of his tormented soul. Nolan reached the line

> "The wretch, concentrated all in self . . . "

and could not go on. He threw the book away and retired quickly to his stateroom. The incident changed him drastically; he became shy and reserved, conscious that the incident had become associated with his legend, and he kept at bay those men who would have befriended him. This was one of the two great crises in his life as a captive. The other came in 1812, during the war with Britain. He offered to fight for his country, but was curtly reminded that he had no country. Should a vessel on which he was kept be posted to the war zone, he was transferred to one in a safer area.

He was aboard one of the most famous of all American warships, the *Constitution*, when on September 29, 1812, she encountered H.M.S. *Java* about thirty miles off the coast of Brazil. The American ship was commanded by Captain William Bainbridge, as humane as he was professionally skilful. The *Java's* opening broadside was devastating; it smashed through the *Constitution's* hull, killing the gunnery officer and scattering many of the crew. The situation was confused and panic was imminent when Nolan grabbed a ramrod, rallied the men and took charge of a gun. During the two-hour battle he did much to restore and maintain morale and no man did more individually to defeat the *Java*, which at the end of the fight was a bloody hulk. Bainbridge sent for Nolan and presented him with his own sword. "Mr. Nolan," he said, "we are all very grateful to you today; you are one of us today. You will be named in despatches." Nolan was too overcome with emotion to say much that was coherent, but Bainbridge's words gave him clear hope of release. The captain not only praised Nolan but is believed to have recommended that his sentence be rescinded, or at

116

least relaxed. Records of any written reply to his suggestions were lost in the Washington fires in 1814, but Nolan was kept under the same conditions as before.

Bainbridge, the renowned Admiral Porter and numerous other senior American naval officers personally petitioned politicians and senior civil servants about Nolan's case. The reply was always the same: no such person as Philip Nolan officially existed, therefore nothing could be done. For authority it had become a kind of game, as captivity often does to the captor. Subconsciously perhaps, the captors wished to see how long the game could be kept alive. The men who refused to admit Nolan's existence had never seen him; he meant nothing to them personally. The situation was without emotional involvement. Nolan was a living example, he was a constant reminder to all American officers that there could be no qualifications to loyalty, let alone denial of it. Nobody has ever attempted to evaluate the influence of Nolan's example on American service morale, but it must have been considerable. Authority was sacrificing one man for the good of the whole and to salve its own pride.

Nolan's punishment continued year after year, decade after decade. Dozens of captains had him as their guest, each one handing him on to the next to put to sea, together with the now rather tattered list of instructions which everybody knew by heart anyway. Nolan aged and dried up. America, of course, was surging forward in many ways. A new generation of Americans was born and few people who had attended Nolan's trial remembered that he was alive, if indeed they were alive themselves. Nolan heard not a word of the great rush to the West, of trail blazing by waggon and train, of political changes. If he himself made any appeals to the government there is no record of them. Probably, after a time he developed a sense of utter resignation which prevented him from taking any further action on his own behalf. He became a legend in the navy, a kind of Old Man of the Sea. During the third decade of his sentence officers and men had given up referring to him by name and spoke of him as "Plain Buttons". He nearly always wore army uniform from which regulation buttons bearing United States insignia had been removed to be replaced by plain brass ones.

On May 11, 1863, fifty-five years after his sentence had begun, Philip Nolan became ill while on board the corvette U.S.S. *Levant* in mid-Pacific. Nolan sent for the commander, Captain Danforth, who saw at once that his elderly guest was seriously ill and dying. Danforth, who had not previously been in Nolan's cabin, saw a large, competent painting of an American eagle—the national emblem—clutching a globe of the world and sheltering it with outstretched wings. Nearby was a map Nolan had made of the United States as it was in 1807. Danforth, a humane man, agreed to Nolan's plea to fill in the map to show him how the country looked in 1863. He answered Nolan's flood of questions about his homeland and later said that he thought Nolan died happier for the information.

He was buried at sea, but whether or not this was ordained by the original orders is not known. Danforth had no option, having no facilities for carrying a corpse a long distance. In any case, Nolan left a brief will asking that he be buried at sea. "It has been my home and I love it," he wrote. In his Bible, Danforth found a text marked with a slip of paper: "They desire a country, even a heavenly: where God is not ashamed to be called their God: for he hath prepared for them a city."

Nolan, in his will, made one last plea. "Will not someone set up a stone for my memory at Fort Adams or Orleans, that my disgrace may not be more than I ought to bear? Say on it, 'He loved his country as no other man has loved her; but no man deserved less at her hands'." If anybody did set up a stone it has gone unrecorded.

Nolan's final sentiments were poetic, but it was not his country that sentenced him to death-in-life. In Nolan's case, as in others, it is all too easy—and all too dangerous—to see the judges as something almost abstract, and therefore impersonal and beyond criticism. But a few men sentenced Nolan and a few more men, spread out over the years, perpetuated his sentence. Somebody, nameless after Colonel Morgan and President Jefferson, insisted that the letter of the sentence be fulfilled. This unflagging remorselessness is one of the greatest dangers that all political prisoners face.

Philip Nolan suffered no physical torture or hunger and, up to a point, no intellectual sterility. He travelled widely and met many men and he lived a healthy life in the open air. But his sentence was one of the cruellest ever inflicted on a human being. One question remains to be answered: why did he not escape? He must have had hundreds of opportunities. He was not guarded and when his ship was in some foreign port he could easily have reached the shore; some captains would have given him time to get well away before raising the alarm and any search would not have been serious, except in the United States itself. Yet, so far as is known, Nolan made no such attempt. The only answer can be that his strict Southern concept of honour kept him on the ship, that he believed he would damn himself by leaving it. By remaining on board and trusting to time, justice and charity he thought he would in due course be honourably released. But the political prisoner can put trust in nothing; for him even hope is dead.

Case History No. 3.   Orsini

Felice Orsini, according to the prosecution at his trial for the attempted assassination of Napoleon III outside the Paris Opera in 1858, was born a conspirator. Orsini's father was an early member of the Carbonari secret society and his own boyhood was spent in an Italy riddled with corruption and oppressed by tyranny—from the Austrians, the clergy in the Papal States and the Bourbons in the kingdom of Naples. Born at the end of 1819, Orsini was only nine when he saw his father arrested and only twenty-three when he was himself first tried for conspiracy.

Anybody courting trouble in Italy in the middle years of the century was almost certain to find it, for a brutal foreign army preserved the power and fortune of the corrupt administrators and it was aided by the secret police, against whose sinister power there was no appeal.

Orsini, though forthright and forcible, was generous in nature and had an acute sense of fun. Completely without vindictiveness, at least in his earlier years, he was dangerously fond of firearms and at sixteen he accidentally killed a family servant. This led to his first flight from authority and his first gaol sentence.

Some Jesuits who knew Orsini said that he was cut out to be a soldier; all his interests and activities were military. He had the soldier's mistrust of politics and a rigid, military code of honour. Joining the Young Italy Movement established by the revolutionary Mazzini, he found an outlet for his zeal and energy. He also studied hard and in June, 1843, he emerged from university as a Doctor of Law with three university diplomas to his credit. Following his arrest on April 30, 1844, Orsini first made his acquaintance with the peculiar rancid smell of prisons. After an initial interrogation he was taken in a closed carriage to a prison at Pesaro, where he was locked in a stifling, solitary cell. Hearing an uproar and clattering of chains, he rapped urgent signals on the wall and found that next door were some of the twenty-one other conspirators who had been arrested at the same time as himself. Seven others had been shot in the back, and these men were about to leave for the galleys, where they would be chained to the walls for life. Life, in most cases, was mercifully short.

Orsini sang to keep his spirits high; when he stopped singing he began thinking and would collapse on his rough bed. This collapse into a sort of defeatist self pity has afflicted many political prisoners in their early prison days.

In July, 1884, he was sent with his captive father to the Papal fortress of San Leo, a tenth-century castle atop a mountain near the ancient city republic of San Marino. It was used to house the most dangerous politicals as well as prisoners awaiting trial for serious offences. At this time San Leo had a reasonably liberal governor and Orsini was able to sketch and read, but the winter cold was so severe that his father became very ill .

Orsini was strangely like Trenck in his flamboyant indiscretion, and his naivety. Concluding that most of his enemies were as liberal as the gaol governor, Orsini announced to his companions in misfortune that the best attitude towards authority was one of firmness and scorn. Disregarding his friends' opinion that this was foolish, Orsini wrote to the Military Commission at Bologna, demanding an immediate hearing of his case and proclaiming that he had done nothing he could regard as shameful. The Commission was irritated—and so was the liberal governor when he unearthed Orsini's plan to escape by bribing the soldiers of the garrison. He pushed Orsini into solitary confinement in a deep, cold dungeon.

Then as now, a political prisoner merited no comfort at all, even in transit. In November, Orsini and others were sent to Rome for trial, travelling in an open cart, shackled together in sixes.

Filthy, vermin-ridden, frozen with the cold, the prisoners huddled together miserably. Once an hour the guards would stop and come up to tug at the chains. This routine was supposedly to find out if the prisoners were tampering with the chains; actually, it was done to impose an agonising wrench on each man's arm in turn. Orsini was learning that brutality is the norm in prison. At night he was lodged in local gaols, often with vicious murderers for company. This brief journey was enough to affect the minds of most of Orsini's companions. Though naturally proud men, the very fact of being in chains and of being kept in common gaols was enough to make them look disgraced, as though they were convicted criminals. Their dignity suffered, but Orsini himself kept his spirit. One morning, as the group was pushed out of a gaol to resume its travels, Orsini shouted, "What are you ashamed of? Are we thieves?" reinspiring the others with defiance.

In Rome he found out that his case would be tried before the Sacra Consulta, a clerical court; he also heard from his counsel, hired by an influential uncle, that the sentence was already decided; the trial (of the others as well as of himself) was merely to give the whole affair a veneer of legality. He would go to the galleys for life.

The citadel of St. Matthew, on the banks of the Tiber, had some secret dungeons which even a fairly thorough inspection would not disclose. Political captives had been lodged in them for centuries and here Orsini and some of his friends were kept. His deep, dark cell received some daylight but no sun and was immediately below the Conferteria, the room where condemned men received the final sacrament before execution. On at least one night Orsini heard somebody pacing restlessly and unevenly overhead. The pacing ceased at dawn and a little later he saw a guillotine with blood dripping from it being carried away outside his window. Orsini spent Christmas in this prison and on Christmas Day was lined up with the other prisoners so that some visitors, the congregation of the Holy Heart of Jesus, could drop coins into their caps. Ordered to thank the visitors for their charity, Orsini did so, wrily one suspects. The captives had been cleaned up for the occasion, as, much later, Christopher Lance, in Spanish hands, was made more presentable for visitors.

After a perfunctory trial in which he was charged, generally, with "conspiracy against all the governments of Italy"—Orsini's sentence was pronounced. It was a sentence of delayed death in the galleys. Orsini and some others obtained some saws from friends in the Young Italy Movement in Rome, but could not deal with their cell bars before they were transferred to another prison, Civita Castellana, a sort of staging gaol where they would wait until death created enough vacancies in the galleys of Civitavecchia. Civita Castellana, a mediaeval fortress, was a foul place, but a hotel in comparison with some other gaols. It held 120 prisoners, mostly long-term captives who had become demoralised, debilitated and savage. Orsini had too strong a sense of justice and was too much of an egotist to ignore all the injustice he saw, and was rash enough to interfere in a quarrel. Six men armed with crude and jagged weapons made in the prison workshop attacked and wounded him in many places but he almost killed one of his assailants.

Orsini had been in Civita Castellana a year when the commandant was told to send men to the galleys; he was afraid of rebellion if he did so openly, so he sent for the prisoners two at a time under the pretext of having them medically examined. When the men did not return the others became suspicious and a riot ensued. Orsini, now head of the captives' committee, walked forward courageously to parley with the commandant under the aimed rifles and cannon of the garrison. He achieved nothing; a captive has no strength from which to parley. Next day the commandant, to prove his power, sent sixty men to the galleys; within three weeks ten of them were dead. Orsini and the others found deliverance in a strange way. The Bishop of Inola, Ferretti, had just become Pope Pius IX, and his first act was to pardon all political offenders. Orsini was free again, having completed an apprenticeship as a political captive.

After a hectic career as a soldier and as a politician Orsini found himself again hunted and was arrested for the fifth time at Hermannstadt, in December, 1855, by the Austrians. Orsini asked not to be sent back to the Papal States, but rather to be shot in Austria. Instead, the Austrians sent him under strong escort to Mantua, centre for the trial and execution of Italian prisoners of state.

At Mantua, on the River Mincio, was the fortress prison of San Giorgio, a massive building with a moat twenty feet deep and twenty-four wide, and heavily garrisoned by Austrian troops. San Giorgio had had a grim history as a prison and its keepers boasted that nobody had escaped from it, though many had tried. Some had jumped into the moat and been pulled to the bottom by the weight of ball and chain. Men had tapped their own veins to write desperate last messages on the walls of their cells before being driven out to execution. Others had died under torture. The strongest cells were reserved for the most prominent troublemakers—men such as Orsini. He arrived there on March 27, 1855, in a pitiable state from hunger, sleeplessness, cold, nervous prostration and dysentery. Almost falling from the van that had brought him, he looked at the soulless building, even more forbidding in the night light, and wondered how he could hope to escape.

He passed through an iron gate, up a long sloping corridor, through a second great gate, sluggishly up a flight of eighty stairs, through a third gate at the top. Here he was received by Francesco Casati, the head gaoler, a man as competent at his business as Saint-Mars. Orsini was thoroughly searched and then locked in a cell, where he found sheets, blankets, a towel and wash basin, a bed with straw mattress and a table and chair. Compared with what Trenck found in his cell, Orsini was fortunate.

Until just before Orsini arrived at San Giorgio the "trials" had been conducted mainly by one of two Austrian captains—Straub, a young, good-looking and sadistic man who would have won acclaim in the SS in the next century, and Kraus, a more subtle but no less terrifying man. Straub often sent men to Cell No. 12, situated at the top of the castle, where the worst tortures were perpetrated on prisoners reluctant to talk. The captives said ironically that the Austrians had chosen this cell because it was nearest to God. The real reason was that it was too far away for the screams to be heard. Flogging was probably the commonest punishment; when it was in progress Casati would stand, watch in hand, and count aloud the number of strokes ordained. Sometimes Straub found the mere threat of being sent to No. 12 sufficient inducement to get a man to talk.

Kraus had a different technique. He had the "Have-a-cigar-old-man" approach; he posed as the prisoner's friend, pleading that he hated violence and would, indeed, see that the prisoner was rewarded, perhaps even released if he were co-operative. Having got what he wanted, Kraus would instantly have his victim taken out to be shot.

At the time of Orsini's imprisonment in San Giorgio things had improved, especially because the British Prime Minister, Gladstone, had condemned such excesses in Italy. European opinion had forced the Austrians to be more humane to their prisoners, so that Orsini found himself treated with reasonable if rigid civility. His interrogator was Baron Sanchez, a clever, merciless and incorruptible man who in 1853 had sent seven Italians to the scaffold and about 130 to the galleys. The technique used by Sanchez was similar to that used by the more suave, subtle Gestapo examiners, by Mussolini's secret police, even by British questioners in more recent years. He asked questions quietly, looked shocked when Orsini made suggestions that he was being victimised, was completely conversational at all times. Sanchez's system was to keep his victim talking until he thoroughly contradicted and implicated himself. But Orsini was astute enough to realise that by talking he could also save himself. He spoke as candidly as Sanchez and at great length, revealing enough of the truth to make his whole story sound true, even giving names when he knew that the people concerned had already been punished. After months of cross-examination it was Orsini who held the initiative, a rare case of the captive calling the tune. Sanchez, who prided himself on being a fine judge of character, saw Orsini as absolutely straightforward—a rabid impulsive patriot perhaps, but not a tricky conspirator. However, the decision was not his; he must send his findings and all the papers to Vienna.

One of the most illogical aspects of prison life is that over the centuries prisoners have been expected to pay for their own keep. Orsini, having only a few shillings when he arrived, would have starved had not Casati supplied him with bread. The gaoler also gave him books—Dante, Byron, Shakespeare. But he refused to bring in books on chemistry and physics. He even noticed one day that Orsini's fingernails were much shorter than the day before, and wanted to know why. The professional gaoler in charge of political prisoners has always had an eye for detail.

The hundred prisoners awaiting trial or execution lived in twelve cells. Cells two, three and four were in a wing overlooking a square, three and four were solitary confinement cells used for special security or punishment. Orsini, as a prime captive, was in three where he was visited by a guard every two hours. The windows were so high that prisoners could not see out; in any case the walls were four feet thick and each window was double-grilled. Below the windows was a sheer drop to the moat, which could not be scaled from the liberty side.

Orsini spent much time thinking about methods of execution. He had been told that straightforward hanging was no longer fashionable, and that the Austrians were now using the *forca*. This was a diabolical form of execution in which the victim stood on a platform with his back against a post; a noose was around his neck and another around his feet, the upper one being attached to a high hook, the other to a revolving cylinder. When the platform was pulled away the pulley stretched the victim and broke his neck. If the contraption failed to work, as it sometimes did, the executioner jumped on the victim's shoulders.

Such thoughts could hardly have helped Orsini's powers of concentration, but he dredged into his mind for information about the great escapes. He had read about Trenck's "rope" of rawhide thongs; he had heard how Latude had climbed his chimney in the Bastille with the aid of a ladder of woven silk, made by unravelling his clothing. He knew, too, about Casanova's escape from the Doge's Palace in Venice, and that Benvenuto Cellini had escaped from the castle of St. Angelo in Rome. And in the end, by sawing through his bars with saw blades sent to him in the binding of books, and by lowering himself 100 feet on a rope of sheets, Orsini himself escaped.

This fabulous adventure won him great acclaim but his next exploit won him even more publicity. Out of tune with other great Italian patriots, such as Cavour and Mazzini, Orsini decided to assassinate the French Emperor, Napoleon III, regarded as the arch reactionary from whom all regal tyrants took their lead. Orsini believed that the elimination of Napoleon would start a revolutionary movement throughout Europe and that it would sweep Italy to independence. He also wanted some great act on which to found a new political party of his own. His story can be briefly told. On January 14, 1858, with three friends, he threw some homemade bombs at the Emperor and Empress in Paris; they escaped but 156 people were wounded and of these eight died. One of the conspirators was sent to the infamous penal colony of Cayenne in the West Indies; Orsini and two others were executed as parricides, though the Emperor and Empress would have pardoned him. Orsini, though in a strait-jacket, sent for books in order to read how Brutus and Cato had met their deaths. He met his own, under the guillotine, with supreme calmness and dignity, probably cultivated in prison.

Orsini is one of the relatively few political captives to have left an account of his experiences, and as it is remarkably objective and

125

without rancour, his testimony is important. In prison his mental activity, much of it connected with his plans to escape, his preoccupation with execution, and his verbal duel with Baron Sanchez, helped to keep him sane. But perhaps not sane enough; his experiences at Mantua could well have influenced him in his decision, which he later regretted, to assassinate Napoleon III.

Case History No. 4.   Dreyfus

The case of Captain Alfred Dreyfus of the French army is too well known in its preliminaries to need recounting here. It is sufficient to say that in 1894, falsely accused of spying for Germany, he was convicted and sent to Devil's Island, most notorious of France's penal settlements.

Appealing to the president of the Chamber of Deputies, Dreyfus was blandly told that "higher interests" than his own prevented recourse to the ordinary means of investigation. In short, he was expendable while the "higher interests" were impregnable.

His prison ordeal began in the Sante Prison, Paris, and as usual on the night of January 17, 1895, he put his cell in order and went to bed, looking forward to a visit from his wife in two days' time. About eleven o'clock he was roughly awakened and told to dress for departure. He was handcuffed, and without even being given time to pick up his spectacles he was taken in bitter cold to a railway station, where rail cars were waiting. The French had special carriages for prisoners who were to be taken to Guiana or New Caledonia, each carriage being divided into narrow cells, barely large enough to accommodate a sitting man. When the door was closed Dreyfus could not stretch his legs; although securely locked in, he had irons on his ankles and handcuffs on his wrists.

He spent a ghastly night in this mobile cell. His limbs were numb, he trembled with fever and in the morning, after repeated requests for food, he was given only a little black coffee and some bread and cheese. About noon the train arrived at La Rochelle, where the guards by devious means managed to attract a large crowd and to induce in them a fever pitch of anger against the "notorious traitor".

At La Palice Dreyfus was put in a longboat for the one-hour trip to the prison on the Île de Ré. Again he froze, his head was "on fire", his hands and ankles were bruised by the irons. Marched

126

through the snow on the island, he was brutally received by the governor who had him stripped and searched. At nine in the evening, "crushed in body and soul", he was put in his cell, adjoining which was a guardroom with a barred window over the prisoner's bed. Night and day two warders, relieved every two hours, were on guard at this window with strict orders not to allow even the movement of a Dreyfus finger to escape them. The governor came to tell him that when he had an interview with his wife, Lucie, he would stand between the couple, so that Dreyfus could not approach his wife or even reach out a hand to her. Each day during his stay on the Île de Ré he was allowed to take a short walk, alone, in a yard adjoining his cell but after each walk he was stripped and searched. Whenever he was in the yard sentries manned the walls. This was complete intimidation.

Extracts from his letters at this time help to reveal the mind of a prisoner:

January 31: . . . What overpowering suffering . . . I read over your letter four or five times, I drink in every word; little by little the written words transformed themselves into spoken words . . . Then, for the last four days, nothing more, gloomy sadness, overpowering solitude . . .

February 3: I have just spent a horrible week . . . I have been without news of you for eight days . . . I have had all sorts of ideas in my fevered brain . . . I have invented all sorts of chimeras . . . I had this single consolation—that your heart was beating in unison with mine . . .

At one of the few interviews she was granted with her husband, Lucie Dreyfus pleaded with the governor to tie her hands behind her back so that she could approach and kiss Alfred. The governor, Dreyfus wrote later, "returned a rude refusal".

On February 21, without warning, Dreyfus was marched from the Île de Ré, taken aboard the prison ship, *Saint-Nazaire*, and placed in the condemned prisoner's cell, a mere contraption of iron bars on the fore deck. The temperature was no more than seven degrees Fahrenheit, but Dreyfus was given nothing more than a hammock without bedding and left without food. The first days of the voyage to the Indies were stormy and he suffered severely from cold and exposure; he was fed on scraps in old meat cans. After fifteen days of this purgatory the ship arrived in the roadstead of the Îles de Salut, where Dreyfus spent four scorching days on deck before being landed and locked for a month in solitary on the Île de Royale.

Several times during this first month Dreyfus believed he nearly went mad; he had "congestion of the brain", by modern diagnosis probably an acute anxiety neurosis. Only remembrance of his wife and children kept him going. He was now taken to the Île du Diable (Devil's Island), a barren rock previously used for isolating lepers.

On the prison ship and again on the Île du Diable Dreyfus felt the "violent almost irrepressible sensation" of being drawn towards the sea; it seemed to him like "some great comforter".

In the first entry of his diary, begun on April 14, he wrote, "I had decided to kill myself after my iniquitous condemnation." This was a natural reaction; thoughts of suicide afflict nearly all politicals in the very early stages of their captivity. "I am afraid," he wrote, "of the terrible moral sufferings I shall have to endure. Physically, I felt myself strong, my conscience was pure and unsullied and endowed me with more than human strength. But my physical and mental tortures have been greater than I expected, and today I am bowed down in body and soul." Dreyfus, like others, came to realise that an "unsullied conscience" can be a handicap.

As early as April 15 he found his nerves had become so sensitive that each new impression, external or internal, produced on him the effect of a deep wound. "Oh," he wrote early in his stay on the island, "if I could only live in my hut without ever leaving it! But I am compelled to take some food or die of starvation."

Repeatedly he complained that the world seemed to have gone back to the Middle Ages; he was especially eloquent about this when all his correspondence was intercepted. For six months he was kept in close confinement, unable to assist those men in France who were working to vindicate his honour.

He was allowed to cut firewood, mostly driftwood, to cook the very tough meat he was issued. All his kitchen utensils were pots of rusty old iron without anything to clean them (until he learned to clean them with ashes) and he had no plates. He suffered violent gastric troubles and had nothing with which to wash himself or his clothes.

This is Dreyfus' own account of a typical day:

"I rise at daybreak, 5.30, light a fire to make my coffee or tea. Then I put the dried vegetables on the fire; afterwards I make my bed, clean my room and begin dressing. At eight o'clock they bring me my rations for the day. I finish cooking the dried vegetables; on meat days I cook the meat. In this way all my cooking is done by ten o'clock, for I eat cold in the evening what is left of the morning meal, as I do not care to spend another three hours in front of the fire in the afternoon. At ten o'clock I breakfast. I read, I work, I dream and, above all, I suffer, until three o'clock. Then I complete my toilet. When the hottest part of the day is over, about five o'clock, I go out and cut wood, draw water from the well . . . At six o'clock I eat what remains from breakfast. Then I am locked up. This is when time hangs most heavily. I have not been able to persuade them to let me have a lamp in my hut. So there is nothing left for me but to go to bed, and then it is that my brain begins to work, that all my thoughts turn towards the frightening drama of which I am the victim, and to my wife and children . . . "

He was weak from poor diet and sleeplessness and the climate was too enervating for him to do any work, even had there been anything constructive he could do. When he could concentrate he studied English and quieted his nerves by sawing and chopping wood for hours on end. There were many times when he had fits of weeping and melancholia aggravated by fever and gastric troubles. When, as occasionally happened, convict labourers were taken to the island to do some work Dreyfus was locked in his hut so that he could not speak with them. Once he spent a full week in his hut for this reason. "Oh, the repulsiveness of mankind! How often there occurs in my mind that exclamation of Schopenhauer, at the spectacle of human iniquity: 'If God created the world, I would not be God'."

He was covered with sores from the stings of mosquitoes and other insects, but "what are my physical sufferings as compared with the horrible tortures of my soul . . . It often seems that my heart and brain will burst. This atrocious life of suspicion, of continual surveillance, of a thousand daily pin-pricks. My blood boils with anger and I am obliged for the sake of dignity to conceal my feelings."

Then, on July 10, 1895, for no apparent reason he was prohibited from walking around his hut and he was put on a convict's diet— about half what he had before with no coffee or sugar. "This is the tomb, to which is added the pain of having a living heart," he wrote. It was virtually a sentence of silence. The guards were coarse and taciturn and opened their mouths only to swear at Dreyfus or to give him some order. He had nothing in common with them and hardly ever spoke to them. He sent to Cayenne to ask for a box of carpenter's tools with which he hoped to fill in some time, but the request was refused. "Why?" he wrote. "Another riddle which I will not try to solve." He was denied everything he asked for.

On December 13 he wrote, "They will certainly end by killing me through repeated sufferings, or by forcing me to commit suicide to escape from insanity." Dreyfus appealed to the President of the Republic. Months later the reply came—"Rejected without commentary". As a political prisoner, he was fortunate even to get such a brief, negative answer.

When he had been on Devil's Island a year he wrote, at four in the morning, "Impossible to sleep. My heart is horribly fatigued by the absence of physical and intellectual activity."

On September 6, 1896, he was told he could not walk within his small area of the island; he could merely walk around his hut. This was an order given for its own sake, probably because it was one of the few the governor could give that he had not already given. The following day he was put in irons. There was no possible chance that he could escape from Devil's Island. The "moral ignominy" worried Dreyfus more than the physical suffering, which was acute enough. On September 9, the commandant, Deniel, visited Dreyfus to explain that the irons were not a punishment but "a measure of precaution", for the prison administration had no complaint to make against him. However, later research indicates that Dreyfus' enemies in Paris had ordered the irons in retaliation for the letters Dreyfus was writing to France, agitating for further inquiries into his case.

The "measures of precaution" extended further than irons. A high solid palisade was erected around the edge of Dreyfus' exercise yard, cutting out much light and air, and an extra guard was posted to watch it. Because of the stockade he did not see the sea for more than two years, although it was only yards from where he lived. No original correspondence, but only copies of it, was to be forwarded. It was feared that Dreyfus might be using code or cipher in his letters, though it is doubtful if Dreyfus had the skill or the guile to concoct a cipher. Another precaution was to put Dreyfus under "double lock" at night, a euphemistic term for chaining him down to his bed. This was another senseless order, nothing short of physical torture.

Deniel always stressed to Dreyfus that he was a simple tool carrying out orders. But Dreyfus later found that Deniel took many measures on his own initiative. This is another constant factor of prison life; the governor and warders always exceed their authority, though this is generally with the tacit approval of higher authority.

He suffered chaining for more than three months. It is quite possible that his political enemies wanted Dreyfus to die, but in the midst of these acute difficulties his "guiding star" dictated his duty. He wrote to himself, "Now less than ever have you a right to desert your post; less than ever have you the right to shorten by a single day your sad and wretched life. Whatever punishments they inflict upon you, you must keep on, as long as your life shall last. You must stand erect before your murderers, as long as you have a shadow of strength, a living wreck, keeping yourself before their eyes, through the indomitable energy of your soul." His soul might have been energetic but his body was suffering. He had fevers, fainting fits, rheumatism, heat prostration, heart attacks, respiratory disorders, diarrhoea, neuralgia, various afflictions of the eyes, "suffocating" fits and haemorrhages.

During 1897 no fewer than ten warders were guarding Dreyfus. The one bright spot was that he had managed to get some books, some sent from France, a few from Cayenne. Only a few survived the voyage, the censor and the pilferer, but Dreyfus devoured them. Shakespeare appealed to him most. "I never knew this great writer so well as during this tragic period; I read him over and over again. *Hamlet* and *King Lear* appealed to me with all their dramatic power."

In June, 1897, since Dreyfus would not die, the authorities arranged a sham rescue attempt and pretended that a rescue schooner was approaching the island. There was much cannon and musket fire and had Dreyfus moved from his hut—he was unchained at this time—he would have been shot. Knowing a rescue to be impossible, Dreyfus did not move from his bed.

The building of the palisade around his hut had made life unbearable; Dreyfus, unoriginally but feelingly, called it a living death.

He had neither air nor light, the heat was torrid and stifling during the dry season, damp and oppressively humid in the wet. Dreyfus was prostrate from lack of exercise and the settlement doctor, who apparently had some spark of humanity, arranged for a new hut to be built. It was on a higher part of the island and was roomier, but again it was encircled by a nine-foot palisade which blocked all view. The new hut was a doubtful blessing, for from the time of its erection Dreyfus found his gaolers more callous; their attitude seemed to vary with the changes in the state of affairs in France. The warders were ordered to ask him loaded questions; when he had nightmares they recorded whatever he uttered in his delirium and Commandant Deniel would then read treason into his words. Every movement the captive made, every change of expression was reported. For instance, Dreyfus sometimes—very rarely—smiled wrily at some further inanity concerning his imprisonment; Deniel would see this as evidence that Dreyfus was expecting rescue. If smoke from a steamer was seen on the horizon all posts were manned and Dreyfus was chained and locked up.

"I know no torture more maddening to the nerves and more insulting to a man's pride than that which I suffered during five years—to have two eyes, full of enmity, levelled at me day and night, every instant and under every condition, and never to be able to escape or defy them; without one moment's respite," he wrote after his captivity ended. He was watched even while he sat in the crude, evil-smelling lavatory.

On September 4, 1897, he wrote to his wife " . . . For a long time I have lived on from day to day, proud when I have been able to hold out through a long day of twenty-four hours. I am subjected to the stupid and useless fate of the Man in the Iron Mask . . . "

By January, 1898, he had thirteen guards constantly on duty; the authorities built a tower above the warders' barracks and equipped it with a Hotchkiss gun to defend the island against attack by Dreyfus sympathisers.

Dreyfus knew nothing of the campaign on his behalf in France; he had only the fragmentary, oblique and infrequent references in his wife's letters that something was being done. He saw his situation "daily becoming more terrible". Persecuted ceaselessly and causelessly, struggling day and night against the elements, the climate and man, he had begun in 1898 to doubt if he would live through his ordeal. "My will was not weakened; it remained as inflexible as ever; but I had moments of savage despair for my dear wife and my darling children, when I thought of the situation in which they were placed."

Even when Dreyfus was returned to France for retrial authority compromised; he was granted a pardon if he withdrew his demand for a retrial. A retrial would have brought to light too many shameful men and their shameful acts. "For me, who had never doubted that justice would be done, what a shattering of all my beliefs!" Dreyfus wrote. "My illusions with regard to some of my former chiefs faded away, one by one; my soul was filled with anguish." The wonder of it was that he had kept his illusions for so long. Eventually, in 1900, his name and reputation were cleared and he returned to the army. In this Dreyfus is unusual among political prisoners; few others have been able to reverse the court's decision, and few others have lived to see justice triumph.

Case History No. 5.   Prisoner "A.D."

One of the most professional and pathetic of political captives was a man known only as A.D. Since this semi-anonymous label may lead some people to conclude that he could be an imaginary character it should be noted that his existence and experiences are attested by German and British publishers and by his biographer, Ernst von Salomon.

A.D. spent twenty-seven years of his life in captivity and in that time lived through three distinct epochs of history, three vastly different political systems. Born in 1901, A.D. was brought up and educated at Plauen, Germany. As a boy he suffered physically and mentally during the violence that followed World War I. Led on by older men, and especially by his fanatically nationalistic school-teacher, A.D. joined the so-called Zeitfreiwillige, an organisation of "temporary volunteers" to protect established institutions and counter the violence of socialism. A.D. wanted to be a forester, but family finances put training out of the question; he settled for the army and signed on for twelve years, at a time when Germany was secretly building up her armed forces in contravention of the Treaty of Versailles.

He liked army life, was competent in its intricacies and in due course he was commissioned. He also met a girl, Charlotte, fell in love with her, and was introduced to her father, a cultured, Communist writer. It was now 1923 and General von Seeckt, re-establishing the German army, was trying to form military alliances with other nations. The political situation was dangerous. Lieutenant A.D., posted to the 12th Reichswehr Infantry Regiment at Magdeburg, was appointed leader of a "reconnaissance detachment", a sort of spy unit. It was A.D.'s job to arrest, inconspicuously, all "politically unreliable" people, such as Communists, and take them to headquarters. It was a grubby, non-military duty—although it was labelled "Military Security Service"—but A.D. was in no position to decline it.

He did not know what happened to the people he arrested, though having once seen a group of them dishevelled, bruised and bleeding, he must have had suspicions. He was too young to realise that political prisoners were fair game for anybody who felt like kicking or beating them; once a man is labelled "an enemy of the state" he has no rights.

A.D.'s moment of truth came one day when he saw on a list of persons to be arrested the name of his girl friend's father. In civilian clothes he travelled to Dresden and warned the man. After this incident A.D. approached his duties in a different way; he began to notice that the people he arrested were quite ordinary and in no way sinister or suspicious in appearance. Among other things he was curious as to why so many school teachers were on his list. Then came a disastrous day for A.D. himself. While examining the books of a man he had arrested he came across a Communist paper which mentioned his own name and described how he had given warning to Charlotte's father. Unfortunately he was with another officer and because of a chain of minor circumstances was not able to destroy the incriminating paper. Believing that the paper, when it was read at headquarters, would destroy his career, A.D. promptly deserted.

Exhausted and hungry, after five days he concocted a story and gave himself up to experience his first interrogation. He also encountered that phrase at once so significant and frightening—"full confession". If he made a full confession, he was told, he would be reasonably treated.

He sent for a defence lawyer, still not realising that in an authoritarian state, few lawyers would run the risk of defending an enemy of the state, no matter how obviously harmless he might be. The lawyer said, "All that's necessary is for me to read your record. You'll get twelve years' penal servitude for treason." He got fourteen years.

A.D. fell a victim to a system of judicial conformity and sterility. In warning Charlotte's father, A.D. had been guilty of no more heinous feeling than love for a girl; he had done what he had because of this love. But the judges felt compelled to find deeper motives.

Like Trenck before him, A.D. found himself the centre of a conspiracy of silence. Nobody at the prison knew why he was there. The gaol authorities did as they were told: they put him in solitary and even refused to allow him to take part in communal exercise, although other men in solitary had this privilege. He did not mind solitary life because he had an even greater dread of communal life. His pride had been profoundly hurt, he felt unclean, ashamed and resentful, and merely wanted to be left alone to lick his wounds in peace.

A.D. was given constructive work—gluing paper bags together. He became obsessed with the idea of smoking, the tobacco having been given to him by the foreman of the firm which employed the prisoners to make bags, but he had no matches. He was uncomfortable and distressed when he realised that somebody was viewing him through the spyhole. However, it turned out to be a helpful trusty who told A.D. how to make fire for his tobacco and how to make contact with the outside world. A.D. scrubbed his cell floor every day, made his bed daily in the prescribed manner, carried out whatever tasks were ordered and from time to time he answered senseless, useless questions—and hoped for "justice".

During the 1920s the League for Human Rights had been formed, an international humanitarian organisation whose self-imposed task it was to investigate cases of illegal and oppressive imprisonment and to alleviate the sufferings of prisoners. A.D. was able to write to the League, which was interested but could do nothing to arouse public interest because—the excuse came once again—the proceedings had been in secret and nothing could be revealed.

A.D., though he did not know it, was undergoing a Dreyfus-like punishment. For reasons too complex to discuss at length, the German army was using him as a scapegoat. To maintain the

135

momentum of its build-up the German army needed the condonation of the French, but the French would not co-operate if they thought Germany was going Communist. They had to be convinced that the German army was the one force in all Germany capable of coping with the Communists, and that it had no dealings with them. At this point A.D. blundered into the situation; his tenuous connection with the Communists could be played up. The army hoped for the death sentence, which would enable them to say to the French, "This is what we do with officers who collaborate with the Communists." So, up to a point the court which tried A.D. was flouting the army in awarding A.D. a sentence of only fourteen years. The court probably reasoned that after such a long period the whole business would no longer matter. But while the Dreyfus case came into the open, that of A.D. did not.

In 1925, when Marshal Hindenburg was elected President, he proclaimed an amnesty for political prisoners and A.D. was transferred to an open prison, where he was to remain in "preventive detention". Conditions were so liberal that men were even allowed to go on leave for two weeks each year, spending it wherever they chose; they merely had to give their word of honour that they would return.

A young social scientist tried to rouse interest in A.D.'s case, but he was frustrated at every turn by the same old story—a case of high treason could not be investigated. A prominent lawyer, Kurt Rosenfeld, both as a representative of the League of Human Rights and in his own right, made great efforts on A.D.'s behalf; he achieved nothing. Even Dr. Kohlsrausch, Dean of the Faculty of Law at Berlin University, appealed on his behalf without success.

A.D. learned much later that whenever his name came up for review between 1924 and 1933, one particular officer in the Personnel Division whom he had known as a captain in 1923 and who had a grudge against him voted against his release.

At Christmas in 1930 the prison governor advised A.D. to go on leave, largely to prevent his prisoner from breaking down altogether. A.D. wanted no sexual diversions, or even the peace of country walks; he travelled to Berlin to see a high official with jurisdiction over his case, but made no progress.

Why did A.D. not attempt to escape? He had opportunities to do so when in the open prison. His biographer, Salomon, says it was because he had given his word of honour to return and that he did not want the privileges of other political detainees curtailed because of any act of his. Also, he must still have cherished the belief that by returning to prison he was proving himself innocent. After seven years in prison a more hardened man would have taken the opportunity to leave the country. A.D. felt that his conduct was the best proof of his being "not guilty", another sign of his optimistic naivety.

He had the misfortune to be in prison when the Nazis took over Germany in 1933. The first time he met SS thugs, they beat him with truncheons, kicked him and forced him to throw his books into a fire. At Sonnenburg he became acquainted with another terrifying word in the vocabulary of prison captivity—re-education. This, at Sonnenburg, consisted of doing everything at the double, and of being woken up for beatings in the middle of the night.

During the period of the Third Reich, the number of "dangerous enemies of the state" arrested increased enormously. The build-up began with professional criminals, or those who had been previously punished three times for the same crime, although they might have been law-abiding for twenty years or more. Then came Jehovah's Witnesses, homosexuals, former members of the Foreign Legion, stateless people, members of the Catholic church and others who did not wish to support the "German church", and many more. Prison space had to be found for these people and the concentration camps were born.

In one of the mass movements of prisoners, A.D. was sent to Buchenwald in 1938. He was strapped on to a wooden stand and flogged soon after his arrival because an official had confused his name with that of some other prisoner who had committed an "offence". For two weeks he could lie only on his stomach.

He also spent about twenty-one days in a dark, cold cell in a bunker without food. This was the standard demoralising process, though it was not necessarily standard in form. Then, his eyes assaulted by daylight, he was pushed into the superintendent's office, which was ornamented with a scroll proclaiming that honour was loyalty. The superintendent took down a whiplike truncheon and beat A.D. into unconsciousness. He was brought to with cold water, had his arms chained together and then hung on a hook. In this agonising position his shins were beaten with the truncheon.

137

He was expected to "confess" though he knew not to what. It was an echo of what had happened to him eighteen years before.

While in Buchenwald A.D. saved a number of men, including Allied officers, from death and when the war ended he became an official. His work was to trace and put under guard all supply camps in Thuringia, and in five weeks he unearthed material worth 1,000 million marks. Later he began a course of training to become a postal official. Then came disaster once again. Two American officers appeared, took him to a camp where a number of industrial war prisoners were being kept and after this to Dachau where he was interned as a witness in war trials. He was a witness not for the prosecution, but the defence, a dangerous role at that time. He was again arrested, interrogated, refused information, treated coldly by both Americans and Germans and finally, weeks later, charged with "violation of the laws and usages of war" in that he had helped to operate Buchenwald prison. When he appeared before the American Military Court in April, 1947, he heard that the prosecution hoped to prove that he had murdered 10,000 men in an experimental block. The Allied officers he had helped were produced as *prosecution* witnesses. Given only ten minutes to plead his case, he was awarded fifteen years' imprisonment and taken to a gaol at Landsberg, without any official statement of the verdict.

A.D., a "dangerous enemy of the state" in 1923, was now a dangerous enemy of the new regime. Some people tried to help him in his new plight but all documents had disappeared. He was four years in gaol, mistakenly and unjustly held, before on December 1, 1950, he was finally released.

He had spent twenty-seven years in prison, under three different political systems, two of which merely "inherited" him. He is the classic example of the principle of prison momentum; having been given a bad name he was compelled to keep it, no matter how little he deserved it. A.D.'s case is extreme, but it does illustrate the danger of trials about which information is suppressed, for the captive cannot then be reached by the forces of reason.

7

Survival

〇〇〇〇〇〇

The point about prison which so few prisoners fail to emphasise is that it is no different in essence from the ordinary world. The basic difference is that in prison everything is concentrated while in normal life experience is diluted. In normal life the callousness, thoughtlessness, selfishness and other human failings and vices are scattered in time and space and there is much to muffle their stings. In the rarefied atmosphere of prison, devoid of mollifying influences, the basic element of all life, the fight for survival, is purified. Many prisoners are loath to concede this point. Frankl, however, is deliberately honest on this subject: " . . . on the average, only those prisoners could keep alive who, after years . . . had lost all scruples in their fight for existence . . . they were prepared to use every means . . . even brutal force, theft and betrayal of friends, in order to save themselves . . . There was neither time nor desire to consider moral or ethical issues. Every man was controlled by one thought only: to keep himself alive for the family waiting for him at home, and to save his friends. With no hesitation, therefore, he would arrange for another prisoner, another number, to take his place in the transport [to the gas ovens]."

Bettelheim says that "in the end most prisoners chose to be sure of their bread rather than their self esteem". The struggle to survive is relentless because, as Levi says, "everyone is so desperately and ferociously alone".

In contrast, Parvilahti, in Butirka Prison in 1945-46, considered his cell-mates "one big family" and noted that the men kept the bread ration of a man absent under interrogation and gave it to him on his return. They also comforted him with an illicit cigarette. But at this time Parvilahti and his cell-mates had been prisoners for a relatively short time.

It is as well to state bluntly that the picture of suffering prisoners uniting in their adversity is generally false. It can exist and it has existed, but not beyond a certain point of oppression. It is possible that the captors would tolerate a degree of camaraderie, but heroic, selfless unity is extremely rare. Indeed, if we are to subscribe to the thesis that self-survival is a powerful instinct, pure charity in a political prison would be unnatural. Even those men who are not *actively* trying to survive at the expense of others find passive means to the same end. The former steal from their comrades, the latter merely refuse to share an illicit turnip. The former will falsely report a comrade for some prison offence in the hope of winning reward; the latter will merely decline to give true evidence to save the reported man from punishment.

In a large room or hut men steal from one another regularly and automatically. This was especially so in the Nazi prisons where a man soon learned to sleep with his head on a bundle made up from his jacket, containing all his belongings from his shoes to his feeding bowl. In political captivity a man must learn to wash with this pitiful bundle held between his knees; to put it down even at his feet invites theft. He must take everything he owns with him every time he visits the lavatory.

Surprisingly little has been written about the serious internal tensions and divisions among prisoners. Even in the literature of Nazi concentration camps this subject is given little attention, rather in the way that selfishness and callousness among prisoners-of-war have been ignored. Social, political and ideological battles raged in the Nazi prisons. The prisoners were probably not aware of it, but in defending their own beliefs and attacking those of others they were helping to keep themselves alive. A man with an interest, even a destructive and selfish one, was much more likely to survive than the man who had given up.

Koestler noted in his diary that he had imagined more solidarity among political prisoners. He was disappointed that so little camaraderie existed, but after a while he could not have been surprised at its absence. The clear-headed Ignotus, denying prison fellowship, critical of the prison-purity that some other prisoners profess, says that "men do not stop deceiving each other because they are sharing the same strawsack". He states that snobbery of all kinds exists among prisoners and, even more bluntly, that "men cannot live without lies, certainly not in slavery".

Political captives often hate and despise one another and keep themselves afloat by kicking others down. Yet when the desperate egoism, forced onto every man who does not want to die in prison, is broken through, it often flowers into "a despairing tenderness"* rarely met with elsewhere. Sazonov seems to have found this feeling.

> Your own sufferings disappear when you consider that all your comrades are suffering just like you. If you only knew how splendid it is to feel yourself a fraction of a tremendous whole; to own nothing whatever of one's own; to own not only no material possessions such as bread or gold, but even to have lost the sense of one's own separateness; to be in a state in which even joy and sorrow are common property. If you could really understand and feel what I mean you would have discovered the secret that keeps us so fresh and green, so little sensitive to what, outside, in freedom, is called personal suffering.

Countless people must have observed that political prisoners *en masse* appear indistinguishable from one another. In photographs and in newsreel films this sameness is striking; some of it can be explained by their hunger, which makes all men lean and bony, and some of it is caused by the shaven heads. But there is more to the sameness than this; prisoners do, in fact, become like one another. Sameness, the attempt to efface themselves so as not to draw unwelcome attentions, is forced upon them. Koestler calls it a "protective coloration". What he means is that each prisoner is expected to play a certain role and instinctively he plays it, fitting into it almost without reasoning. Vrba knew "that those who were different died in Auschwitz, while the anonymous, the faceless ones, survived". Men become "prison types" to protect themselves from being singled out by the authorities; but this reaction also makes it easier for the staff to think of them as sub-standard beings, as human animals. This is why so very little sympathy exists between guards

* Iulia de Beausobre's phrase.

and guarded. The prison environment is a tremendous moulding force; those who survive their captivity need time to readjust to normal life, just as a man fresh from the armed forces does.

Mrs. de Beausobre's reaction to the early days in prison was to lie as flat as possible, effacing herself, pretending that the evil eye was not watching her through the spyhole. Such self-effacement has its dangers, for it can produce a completely submissive, negative personality. Still, it is better than torture and death. One of the most pathetic sights in a prison is the front row at inspection time. Front-row prisoners are more noticeable, are nearest to hand and are easiest to beat for any minor infringement of regulations.

In ordinary civilian life most people are members of a vast group which we could call the Drab, sandwiched between the Dominant and the Doomed. But among political prisoners there is no middle group. The man who can learn to become a Dominant in one way or another—and this could range over a vast field, from becoming a kapo to exploiting his body as a homosexual—has a good chance of surviving. The weak, the inept, the careless, the melancholic, the ingenuous are those who are "selected" for extermination or extra work or suffering. Most experienced politicals believe that the Doomed rarely last longer than three months under Nazi conditions or two years under the conditions of south-eastern Europe. Levi calls these people of weak survival prospects "non-men".

In the first year of captivity in the Soviet Union about a third of the prisoners die, through sheer inability to withstand the conditions. Ekart believes that for the first year the prisoner is so depressed and "so morally and physically outraged" that his powers of observation are greatly reduced and limited to his physiological reactions.

Vrba says that though physically he was probably fitter than most he had to fight to keep up his morale. "The smell of death, the sight of walking skeletons, the constant degradation all pressed in on me . . . " He came near to breaking when he met a column of shambling Slovakian women, starving, filthy and beaten, including his own seventeen-year-old cousin.

An important part of survival is the ability not to notice, which means pretending not to notice, what is going on. It is dangerous and sometimes fatal to observe a guard maltreating another prisoner; to show any emotional reaction to such an incident is even more dangerous. For such an offence the SS might goad a man to suicide or murder him in the punishment bunker. In the fellowship of the lost, there are many little tricks to be learnt in the battle for survival. A man learns how to get hold of a bowl before they are all gone; he learns to find a place in the centre of a marching group, for the men on the outside catch most of the truncheon blows, and to recognise which pile of sleeping straw is the deepest.

Levi felt that he could not resist and therefore could not survive because he was not "made of the stuff of those who resist. I am too civilised, I still think too much, I use myself up at work." After only one week in Auschwitz he lost all instinct for cleanliness, though he may have recovered it later when he realised that it was one way towards holding on to life. Often it was the men who forced themselves to go through the rituals of shaving, polishing their shoes and doing their hair who survived. What these motions cost them in effort only they can know. "Our wisdom," says Levi, speaking for the old hands at Auschwitz—they had survived five months—"lay in not trying to understand, not imagining the future, not tormenting ourselves as to how and when it would all be over; not asking others or ourselves any questions."

After a man learns to live in a prison or a concentration camp his chance of survival increases greatly. He is not only less likely to die from a psychological loss of desire to live; his knowledge also gives him more physical resistance to exhaustion.

Education had taught Trenck to despise death, so he defeated it. Ekart came to understand the vital importance of moral courage. "As long as a prisoner retains his will to live, and to overcome hunger, torture and exhaustion, he survives. But the moment this is lost, all is lost and the end comes quickly."

A captive's collapse often begins quite suddenly. One morning he may simply refuse to get up and is content to lie in his own excreta. Blows and threats have no effect and he soon dies. When a man loses all hope for the future his body seems to lose its resistance as well and becomes vulnerable to disease.

Prychodko at Tansha in 1940 saw many beaten men. "It was a most distressing sight to see these scarecrows of prisoners . . . with heavy feet . . . dirty, tattered and deathly pale . . . a mass of hopeless human beings, degraded, walking more like robots than men . . . Many thousands of people of high cultural standing lost their individuality, their hope for the future and all semblance of normal human beings."

Eugene Heimler, a prisoner in Auschwitz, says, "When self-respect is lost, then faith is lost, and when faith is lost, man becomes a number without a name."

Despite all the factors that militate against it, a political has a remarkable capacity for adaptation, for creating by abstract and concrete means a sort of niche for himself. Even in the chaos of the big concentration camps this was possible. Most men find it necessary to assert their personality in some way. In normal life one man may do this by buying a motor car of a particular type, another by collecting stamps. In prison, in a large cell with many other people, it is done in more simple and subtle ways—by hammering in a nail above a bunk to hang his shoes on, by coming to terms with his neighbours in the cell or hut, by making some secret mark on a bunk, by making an effort to understand and conform to the un-written laws and practices of the hut, by using particular skills as a carpenter or cobbler or doctor or philosopher. By these means the prisoner weaves a cocoon of comfort which, though slight, protects him more than his oppressors know.

Prisoners generally try to avoid making decisions or using any sort of initiative. Most captives develop a strong feeling of Fate, and a conviction that any attempt to influence it will result in even more trouble. This resignation is another form of defence mechanism. The prisoner prefers to let Fate make the choice for him; then, if the choice is fatal, he cannot blame himself for the disaster. But making decisions is vital if a man is to preserve some independence of mind, a spark of spiritual freedom, even in the worst conditions. Some men achieve this high degree of character and personality, though all political prisoners agree that their number is few. Only a man who has overcome some great disability can appreciate the satisfaction of a prisoner who masters his surroundings or some aspect of them, such as the pain of torture.

Most plans to commit suicide are not carried out, but by making "decisions" to take his life a man achieves a remarkable sense of peace. If he is lucky enough to get hold of a piece of sharp tin or a dagger of glass, he feels even more confident because he can tell himself that if he feels like it he can put an end to his suffering.

A paramount decision, at least in Begin's opinion, is "to renounce all things": principally, the political prisoner must be able to give up the idea of complaining. Complaining gains nothing, only giving satisfaction to the oppressors, but it is difficult to control. Rupert believes that it is better for family separation to be complete, and that a prisoner is much better able to stand captivity if he gives up all hope of ever again seeing his family.

Bettelheim helped himself to survive Dachau and Buchenwald by systematically observing and analysing his own behaviour and that of the people around him. This gave him a more objective and detached interest in his ordeal, and at the same time he gained much emotional relief and self respect through giving his experience a purpose and meaning.

Similarly, Heimler probably survived Auschwitz and three other camps because he created a purpose for himself, nothing less than an intention to record the tragedy of Auschwitz. Dedicating himself to the role of eye-witness he watched and observed, remembered and absorbed, and won his victory. It would be too much to say that his sense of purpose protected him from bullets and the gas chamber, but perhaps it played a part in doing so.

Certainty of acquittal has a major bearing on survival. Man is an incurable optimist and a political prisoner, knowing he has broken no law, can hope that his innocence will in the end release him. But once his sentence is pronounced, definite hope fades and with it the will to resist. There are innumerable cases of politicals surviving years of frightful treatment, to succumb in months or even weeks after a sentence has been pronounced.

There are many survival aids. Frankl learned, in the very depths of his suffering, that "the salvation of man is through love and in love". While hard at work in freezing weather, hungry and with little hope of physical salvation, he clung to the image of his wife and from it drew unassailable strength. He even had conversations with her*.

Some prisoners manage to hold on to their self respect by convincing themselves that they are regarded as important; otherwise, their reasoning goes, they would not have been singled out for punishment.

Some men owe their survival to the conviction that someone else's troubles are more serious than their own. This is the principal

* But she died in a prison camp, as did Frankl's parents and brother.

consolation of the disabled. On the other hand those politicals who become convinced that nobody's sufferings could be worse than their own are dangerously close to extremes of self pity.

When she was in a state of depression or torment, Iulia de Beausobre would "slip away into Samarkand". She had spent a happy year with her husband in Samarkand and now she revisited the city: she felt during these self-induced hallucinations that she was living in Samarkand, breathing the air of the snow-capped hills, touching the petals of desert tulips, hearing the mountain eagles.

But although hallucinations of many types help to keep a political prisoner sane, they can also send him over the line into madness. Use of the mind can easily become abuse of it. This is different from the selective amnesia which some prisoners develop and by which they are able to obliterate distasteful areas of memory, or even pleasant areas which can cause acute distress.

Many prisoners reach a state of near-hypnosis in which the real cannot be separated from the unreal; they become automatons, obeying without questioning, acting without thinking, enduring pain and immense effort without being conscious of it. Pellico learned that a man can make his state of mind independent of place. "Control our imaginations and we can be happy almost anywhere." Pellico was not always successful in putting this theory into practice and many prisoners, such as those held by the Nazis and those gaoled by the Rumanians between 1950 and 1960, would hotly dispute it, but Paloczi-Horvath, while in Gyujofoghaz, wish-dreamt that he was invisible and that his body in its invisible state could penetrate through thick walls.

Another path to survival lies in a self deception that enables a man to see himself as a hero rather than a humiliated nonentity. He returns from an interrogation with the boast that he "gave as good as he got" or that he "put the interrogator in his place". He may even claim to have told the questioner "what he thought of him". These boasts are often expressed in standardized clichés. Those of the man's cell-mates who have themselves been interrogated know that all this is vainglorious bravado, and the captive knows they know it, but this does not detract from his sense of well-being. Following some humiliation inflicted on a group of prisoners, each man in the next few days will recall some brave gesture made or bold word spoken. Where cowardice is compulsory, as it is in a political prison, it is only human to want to salvage something from shattered self esteem. In the same way, as Bettelheim points out, the dreams of many prisoners in Nazi hands combined aggression and wish fulfilment in such a way "that the prisoner was able to revenge himself on the SS".

In a practical way, Vrba learnt in the clearing house of looted property at Auschwitz to steal only what somebody else dropped. It was not safe to steal what you yourself dropped, for kapos and SS would converge with clubs. But while they beat the careless worker others could scoop up fragments of food or other things.

Vrba, only eighteen when he was imprisoned in Maidanek, had wit enough to learn the art of survival quickly. He made each mistake only once. While working he spoke to the man next to him; a kapo clubbed him. Vrba did not speak again. He noticed that a prisoner who cried out in pain and protest when being beaten was much more savagely handled than a man who could stay silent; Vrba stayed silent. He learned not to run from punishment, for a pack of kapos would chase and club a running man. He learned how to steal a potato when sent on duty to the kitchens. And his ever-present intention to escape made him seize an opportunity to be transferred from Maidanek to Auchswitz.*

Information is another aid to survival. If news is constantly available prisoners' morale is much higher. The "telegraphists" in a prison through their self-appointed duty, are helping themselves as well as others to survive.

Begin came into contact with several of them in his gaol. Here the telegraphists were dependent on the wind. If there was a favourable wind, the fragmentary news reached the headquarters of the "telegraphic service", two cells on the top floor whose windows faced the far-off city square. When the news was received, it was transmitted "lengthwise" and "breadthwise" to every communal cell: "lengthwise" with the aid of the water pipe, and "breadthwise" by means of the walls. In this technique one tap stood for a "dot", two successive taps meant a "dash". All the letters of the alphabet were, according to an agreed key, dots or dashes or a combination of

---

* He was lucky. On November 3, 1943, the Germans drove the 17,000 prisoners of Maidanek into ditches and machine-gunned all of them to death. This operation, "Harvest Festival", was their way of closing down the prison camp.

both. Begin claims that there is an internal "telegraph" in every Russian prison. The telegraphists work in perpetual danger. When the time comes for receiving the news or transmitting it, one man crouches next to the door, and a few paces away, a second guard stands upright, to forestall a surprise visit from the warder and to obscure the Judas window.

Of all men, the Greek prisoners seem to be the toughest, the ones most likely to survive. There were some in Auschwitz. Levi describes them as " . . . those admirable and terrible Jews of Salonica, tenacious, thieving, wise, ferocious and united, so determined to live, such pitiless opponents in the struggle for life". In a camp of mixed nationalities it is the Greeks who rule the roost in cells and huts, in the squares and yards, in the kitchens and the stores. Even the German guards respected the Greeks. They nearly always control the markets and the monopolies. Even in the worst of Nazi concentration camps there was a barter market with regular dealers in their regular stalls and casual traders on the fringes. In the market a torn piece of cotton cloth, probably torn from a shirt tail, could be exchanged for bread, bread for soup, soup for an illicit pill of some kind, a piece of tobacco for a carrot, a carrot for a piece of turnip, a safety pin for the cotton cloth. Fillings from gold teeth were often used as currency, but only for major transactions. Anything that could be stolen by men on working parties would find its way into the market—soap, nails, tools, candles, pieces of wire, matches, grease—a useful commodity as it was rubbed into shoes to make them a little more comfortable. Such markets were a material aid to survival.

It is sometimes possible for a man of cold courage and self-discipline to impose his will on a crowded prison of political prisoners. The prime requirement is a sense of purpose so ruthless that the man concerned shows no more kindness to himself than to others. A smart appearance is essential, or at least a smartness and cleanliness which stands out in contrast to the other prisoners. This draws attention to him, a fact which most prisoners would regard as dangerous. But this particular man must also have the ability to look suitably humble in front of his captors and suitably proud before his comrades. He is courteous to all. He becomes a model prisoner, first to "volunteer" for a distasteful task and first to form the queue, though this is not a favourable spot when soup is being served for it is then at its most watery. Through these and other subterfuges he will be remembered when somebody is needed to take charge of a prisoners' working party, to make a secret report on illegal activities of his fellow prisoners or to supervise some activity. This type of individual—individual in the real sense—is often a humanitarian, and uses what he gains for the general good.

Edith Bone's path to survival was probably unique. Her chief defence against her captors was her sense of her own intellectual superiority and of her gaolers' inferiority. She treated them with profound contempt; they did not like this but they could do nothing about it. They regarded this extraordinary woman as insolent and incorrigible, which she was. "Each new guard had to be taught that I would not stand any rudeness, would not address any of them in the prescribed terms of respect, and was a holy terror in general, so that conflicts with me were best avoided . . . My life in this prison I regarded as a battle I had to fight with these very inferior people . . . There was an element of sport in this." Within a year she had developed "complete immunity to anything any of my interrogators might say". In Budapest Central Prison she even took to prescribing for herself, and scared the medical orderlies into bringing her the drugs she wanted. She demanded—and was given—butter, milk, sugar and rusks at one period.

She undermined the morale of her guards in many ways. At various times she refused to get out of bed, to eat, to call her guards "sir", to do exercises. She was rude to everybody from prison governor to prison doctor and her captivity was one long refusal to be intimidated. Her size had a certain effect; on admission to prison she weighed fourteen and a half stone. She declined to clean her cell, insisting that it be done for her. For eighteen weeks she even refused to speak Hungarian and when the governor confronted her she greeted him with "Thug! Assassin! Coward! Murderer!"

It had been decreed that Dr. Bone could neither see other prisoners nor speak to them. However, she overcame the first part of the ruling by making her own spyhole through which she could see what was happening in the corridor and outside some of the adjoining cells. This took a very long time but Dr. Bone was a persevering woman. However, at no time did she have personal contact with fellow prisoners, although in 1956 she taught some of them English, French or German by correspondence.

149

One of her battles was the right to a haircut. When she was not given one in two years she took each hair in turn and snapped it off; the operation took three weeks and resulted in badly cut fingers. The next hair-tearing took two weeks, but after a year she was allowed to have it properly cut. Another battle of months resulted in Dr. Bone's winning a comb.

She did not always have her way. Unable to get warm clothing or bedding in the winter of 1954-55, she sewed two blankets into a sleeping bag—a forbidden practice—and spent most of the winter in bed in what felt to her like a state of suspended animation. She could not read because her hands were too numb to hold a book.

But even Dr. Bone's will and philosophy began to crack after seven years, not from the length of her captivity or the rigours of imprisonment but from the uncertainty engendered by repeated rumours of release and amnesty.

Raphael Rupert saw Edith Bone at this time without knowing who she was. He and other prisoners waved to "this dignified old lady . . . and she gracefully acknowledged our greeting".

Some prisoners learn not only how to survive, but how to prosper. This was especially so in the complex hierarchy of the gigantic Nazi sorting centres, such as Auschwitz, where the great piles of belongings of exterminated Jews were classified. Vrba established himself as a reliable messenger in this macabre storehouse and won many privileges, concessions and gifts from appreciative kapos. He was badly beaten one day when a Nazi overseer intercepted a present of chicken, chocolate and perfume which Vrba's kapo was sending by him to his girl friend, a woman kapo. Vrba was himself a black market commodity; a kapo bought him from his block chief for a lemon. The kapos had their own rooms in each barracks and were able to provide their friends with good meals. Vrba says that in Auschwitz they even cooked steak and chips on their stoves.

Vrba made such influential friends that he managed to survive a serious bout of typhus. This was extraordinary, for men with the slightest trace of typhus or any other serious disease were killed with an injection of phenol. That he could be hidden and nursed until he regained some of his strength was testimony to the power of the Auschwitz underground, for which he later became a courier. But he was extremely lucky, for there is generally no compassion in prison. A weak man is a liability and there is no point in cultivating him.

Some prisoners try to survive by relieving their misery in drunkenness. They crave liquor for its power of inducing forgetfulness, but since it is rarely available they must resort to substitutes. One is eau de cologne, which can occasionally be procured in traffic with free citizens; prisoners in Germany, the Soviet Union and France report having found it a mild intoxicant. In the Soviet Union during 1942-45, much anti-freeze was imported from the United States for use in tractors and other vehicles. The containers were plainly labelled POISON but many prisoners drank it; they died within twenty-four hours from a complete breakdown of the kidneys. A favourite intoxicant is chloral hydrate, which is constantly stolen from prison pharmacies; prisoners call it "dry spirits". Overdoses cause symptoms of paralysis which can last for up to ten months. Elinor Lipper knew many prisoners who drank varnish, which was invariably fatal. Everything prepared with an alcohol base, such as belladonna, ammonia, and even peppermint, must be securely locked up or it will disappear. One man in a Soviet prison camp drank the alcohol in which the hospital was preserving laboratory specimens of various humans organs. It is possible for a patient in a hospital to obtain cloth saturated with ether, which can be inhaled under the blankets to produce ether intoxication.

Survival is not necessarily dependent on physical fitness. Healthy men sometimes break down physically before the thinner, weaker men; the healthy ones complain about their aches and pains more than the others do and they are the ones who try to see the doctor. The man who has suffered from various disabilities and who has learned to live with them is often better off than the robust man, who is alarmed by strange symptoms. Subject to several qualifications, it may be suggested that the best age to become a political prisoner is the early forties, when both body and mind have become mature.

8
Work

◊◊◊◊

In the public imagination the most frequent labour imposed on common law prisoners is the making of mailbags, whereas political captives are slaves in Russian salt mines. There is enough truth in this theory to make the respective labours typical of the whole. Another generalisation is also valid—that the greater part of the work done by politicals is as arduous as it is aimless.

During the earlier part of his imprisonment the political prisoner is not given any work to do, beyond cleaning his cell or a share in cleaning the prison. One of the first gaol tasks Mrs. de Beausobre had was to clean out the washroom; this meant washing down the walls, the floors and the basins, polishing the taps, cleaning the lavatory pans. There was no brush and she had to do the work with her hands and a few bits of rag and some sand.

While a prisoner is under interrogation—which may last for years—the officials responsible for him do not want him to be able to take his mind partly off his troubles by forgetfulness in labour. Usually, not until his case has been finalised and sentence passed is he put to work. Under the Nazi regime, with hundreds of thousands of people involved, mere arrest was finalisation in itself and prisoners were put to work at once. This was pure slave labour, as is much labour in parts of the Soviet Union.

Much prison work must be pointless or it is not punitive. If it were constructive and reasonable it would be some consolation towards the wasting of years of human life, but to make it so would be to help a man retain his dignity and this, in authority's view, must be avoided. This is why piles of rocks are moved from one place to another, why stacks of timber are taken apart and then rebuilt, why great heaps of sand are laboriously carted backwards and forwards. In Janowska in 1942, Wells saw a group of men forced to carry a truck body round and round in aimless circles while guards beat them over the heads and shoulders.

Common criminals, apart from making mailbags, bind books or make boots. Politicals are given no such satisfaction of labour for a purpose, though in the Spielberg at the time of Pellico's stay some prisoners were put to work making stockings from wool, preparing surgical dressings for the army's use and sawing wood. Burney was asked to fold and glue cellophane bags, but could not concentrate on the task sufficiently well to produce neat envelopes and was glad to abandon the task.

The Nazis used their prisoners for a variety of tasks, giving them starvation rations but working them beyond the limit of endurance. They were leased out to various industrial concerns making everything from armaments to fertilisers. They loaded and unloaded railway wagons, laid cement, dug ditches, erected buildings. They even built much of their own prisons and prison camps. At Buchenwald* they had to dig stone from a local quarry and carry it back to the site on their shoulders. Later they had to pull heavy iron waggons, and were ordered to sing as they worked. They built the six-mile road to the dump—the "Street of Blood"—and the railways which ran alongside it. New prisoners, brought by rail or road, were disembarked at a certain point from which they were whipped into prison along "Flog Walk".†

*Buchenwald would have been noted for its position if not for its infamous activities. Goethe knew the site of Buchenwald long before it was a prison. In his day, and indeed until 1938, the area was a beautiful beech forest high on the Ettersberg, north-west of Weimar. The poet liked to rest under a great oak in the forest and around this oak Himmler built his prison. Bitter winds blew into and through the prison square, through the rows of huts. The narrow gate of steel bars was ornamented by a plaque bearing the prison's motto—"To Each His Own".

† There is a common misconception that identical conditions existed in all the Nazi concentration camp-prisons. This is not so. For instance, not all camps were extermination centres. Buchenwald started as such a place but became a work camp in which many prisoners were well clothed and well fed. In some camps the SS allowed chaos to reign while in others there was order and some purpose.

During the Nazi wartime regime one of the busiest industries for politicals was disposing of the corpses of murdered captives. It is a difficult task to get rid of many thousands of bodies, and politicals were used to burn or bury corpses, and to crush to powder the bones that did not burn. Sometimes they disposed of more than 2,000 in a day.

Other prisoners were used to operate the gas chambers in which captives were murdered and the ovens in which the bodies were incinerated. Thousands were needed to sort and classify the millions of articles the Nazis seized from their victims. This work at least gave the prisoners opportunities to steal things which could save their own lives—food, medicine and items useful for trading and for bribery.

That a prisoner was considered fit to work was some guarantee of his survival. Periodically the SS held inspection parades to decide which men were fit to work and which ones should be exterminated. The decision was as much a matter of caprice as of medical opinion, since often all the men paraded were in the same state of gaunt malnutrition and exhaustion. In the Soviet Union work-selection committees periodically tour transit prisons to allocate captives to various areas. Frequently the captives are paraded naked, while gaol doctors advise the commission on their state of health and work potential, that is, whether a man is best suited for lumbering, mining, digging canals and so on.

The plenitude of labour means that no great care need be taken of prisoners sent to labour camps. Forced to board railway trucks and then locked in, thousands have starved or frozen to death en route. Many prisoners, over the last century, have even been forced to walk to Siberia. Such a journey takes as long as two years and claims many lives. Countless captives die of cold or hunger in the great wastes of northern Russia and Siberia.

The Communists believe that no man is a human being until he does some productive work for the community; this is the concept of the labour camps. But the gulf between concept and practice is ludicrous.

The most exhausting labour in the Russian wastes is fetching wood in winter. The men stand up to their knees in snow, so that it is difficult to move. Huge tree-trunks, cut away with axes, sometimes fall on the prisoners, killing them on the spot. Clad in rags, with no mittens and with only thin shoes on their feet, hardly able to stand for weakness caused by under-nourishment, their hands and whole bodies are frozen stiff in the bitter cold. The minimum daily task for four men is to cut, split and pile four cubic sajenes (a sajene is about two yards), and until they have done this they are not allowed to return to the camp. An extra hardship attached to all outside work is that if the prisoners do not get through their minimum task on time and return to camp punctually they get no dinner.

The Soviet prison camp system uses the donkey-and-the-carrot principle. If a man can do more work then the norm he can win himself an extra ration; however the system often defeats itself because, in driving himself beyond the limit, the prisoner often falls *short* of the norm, in which case he is given less food. He then embarks on a desperate attempt at furious physical activity which his undernourished body cannot take. In short, he is driven to commit suicide. In a temperature of minus sixty degrees Fahrenheit death is never very far away.

In some work camps in Siberia and the Russian north, prisoners live only in tents, although they make these warmer by thick walls of snow. Their one privilege is that they may use as much wood as they wish to stoke their stoves—provided they cut it in their own time.

Hard labour in Russian prisons, as distinct from labour camps, varies from stone-breaking in the case of men without any intellectual skills to translating for those with linguistic ability. It is quite possible for a group of three or four men collectively to write twelve languages, and the Russians keep such men busy translating everything from spy novels to foreign service magazines and guidebooks, all of which is fed into the insatiable maw of the intelligence machine. The Soviet system provides for payment of "hard labour", but a proportion is deducted for keep, taxes and other "services".

The Communist satellite countries model their treatment of politicals on the Russian system. Hungary, for example, deducts eight per cent of a political's wage for National Health Service contribution. With whatever remains, the captive is permitted to buy the essentials—toothpaste, toilet paper and even, perhaps, sugar and vegetables. But this is only in principle, for so many officials have a hand in keeping the prisoners' accounts that the money is methodically stolen.

Prisoners with special qualifications, such as doctors, nurses and linguists, often find work commensurate with their skill and live useful lives. The doctors, though working with inadequate and obsolete equipment and constantly under pressure from officials not to "pamper" prisoners, achieve astonishing results. Linguists are at least able to practise their languages, though the work they are given is often sterile and pointless. But these professional people still live an uncertain existence. The doctor today can be the woodcutter tomorrow. A man's training does not guarantee his security in a prison. In any case, such specialised work is for the few. The great majority of those who are put to work dig and chop and lift and carry, working on roads, canals and railways, in mines and forests.

Lack of opportunity to use his brain can have strange effects on a man. After seven years without writing a word, Rupert found it difficult to compose a postcard message for his family when the Russians, at one time, relaxed regulations and allowed foreign prisoners to write home.

Prisoners could do much useful, if hard work, in more congenial surroundings if authority did not have its own motives for keeping them out of sight. To expose them to the public eye might invite comment about their deplorable condition. Not that this worried the SS or the great numbers of the German public who saw the pitiable concentration camp workers. Many prisoners note in their memoirs that civilians with whom they came into contact outside the prisons gave them neither bread nor sympathetic glance. A simple law was at work: if a man looks like an animal, it is easy to believe that he is an animal and to work him as a beast of burden.

9

Time-Filling

○○○○○○○○○

The sheer physical filling-in of twenty-four hours a day is taxing to intellect and galling to patience. No prisoner has more feelingly expressed the tedium than Levi, who says that time passes "drop by drop". Indeed the continuous dripping away of life has somehow to be dammed, and most prisoners try to channel it in some way. A prisoner finds if essential to have a boundary which will make time finite and comprehensible.

In prison time seems to move in inverse direction to time in normal life. For the ordinary man, no matter how dull his life, time moves from past through present to future. For the prisoner, time escapes from future to past, rather like thick molasses oozing from a hole in a drum and seeping downhill. The prisoner tries not to think about the passing of time, for if he does, he becomes depressed by the irrecoverable days that have been stolen from him.

Jawahawal Nehru, imprisoned by the British in India, found that in prison he grew retrospective and, "as the present is dull and monotonous and full of unhappiness, the past stands out, vivid and inviting".

Koestler is one of the very few captives to try to analyse the passing of time and the only one to come close to an explanation. Aware that it was passing but not knowing how, he tried to *see* it passing by staring at the second hand of his watch, which he was fortunate in being allowed to keep. He stared at it until his eyes watered. He was struck by the truth that his prison days and weeks were moving more rapidly than time had ever moved for him before. It dawned on him "that those days which, owing to their uneventfulness and dreariness seem longest shrink to nothing as soon as they have become the past, precisely because of their uneventfulness". Conversely time full of occurrence, of crowded hours and minutes, may appear to pass quickly at the time but in retrospect it is very long. Blank days are no weight on the memory, eventful days do have weight.

However, whatever a man's analysis of the phenomenon of time, it still has to be lived through. Some men, such as Burney, discover an innate talent for becoming anchorites, and in the very early days of their prison life establish a routine by which they exist for years. Burney, in fact, thought that he found the secret to living in prison: to dream of pleasant things when there are none real to be enjoyed and to make the most of the few real pleasures. Burney found patience to be a matter of anticipation. A man did not suffer the passing of empty time but rather the slowness of the expected event which is to end it. "The patient mind is fixed on a future happening, not on present inactivity."

Paloczi-Horvath calls impatience the greatest enemy of prisoners. He says that in one cell, which he shared with many people, he "craved all sorts of actions. I turned and tossed . . . I had to exercise the utmost self-control . . . I wanted to run and run . . . "

But this natural sense of escapism must give way to practical methods of time-filling. Prisoners resort to one of four main methods—the physically creative, the physically active, the intellectual, the imaginative. I am not here discussing physical labour performed for the prison authorities but that voluntarily carried out by the prisoner in his cell.

Physical creativity is centred on making things from the few available raw materials. French prisoners-of-war in Britain during the Napoleonic wars created beautiful objects, such as ships, jewel boxes and ornaments from bone. And in many eras prisoners-of-war have found satisfaction in carving wood. But the political rarely sees a piece of bone or wood and must resort to lumps of dough kneaded from his precious ration of bread. With patience and persistence, prisoners produce an extraordinary array of articles.

Edith Bone probably made more use of bread than any other prisoner. For instance, she made an abacus that enabled her to make calculations up to a million million; she made table mats, skittles and little statuettes. But her great feat was her printing set of 4,000 bread-letters and compositor's case with twenty-six compartments. She had no writing materials at the time but with her printing set she could set out poetry on her table. The abacus enabled her to assess her English vocabulary of 27,369 words, after which she tested her vocabulary in her other languages. She knew many swear words and periodically gave her gaolers the benefit of her knowledge.

Parvilahti knew a colonel prisoner who was an artist in dough. This man worked the bread in his hand for hours like modelling wax, kept it in a damp rag overnight and next morning resumed his kneading. After a few days it was clay-like and from it the colonel formed different sized buttons for his greatcoat, tunic, and trousers. He dried these buttons for several days in a cool spot on the floor, then moved them to a slightly warmer place and finally put them to dry beside the hot teapot every time the prisoners were served their tea. Having quite dried the buttons, the colonel began careful grinding, first against the mortar in the wall, then against the sole of a boot and finally with a bit of cloth. With meticulous care he spent scores of working hours on a couple of dozen buttons, all exactly the same shape, regular, rounded and shining, and almost the same colour as the cloth of his uniform. He asked a guard for needle and thread and sewed the buttons carefully into place. After this, says Parvilahti, his bearing was "very erect and he reminded one far more of a colonel than many of his colleagues still in the service".

Parvilahti saw cufflinks made out of bread by the same method. A Polish prisoner made beautiful small crucifixes out of bread and sold them to other Catholics. Cell facilities for colouring these articles were few, but from the window-frames the sculptors could scrape off some of the blue blackout paint, from the walls white lime, and black soot could be got by burning bits of rag.

In June, 1945, Thomsen was in prison in Moscow with a German, Heinz Remlinger, who had made a pencil—a remarkable feat. To do this he first broke a piece of iron from his bed and ground it with stones brought from his exercise yard into a knife. With the knife he cut several slices of wood from the back of his cell table. During his interrogations he was often given real pencils with which to write, and he sometimes managed to break the points and keep the pieces of lead. The lead he put into his splinter pencil, keeping the pieces in position with soap and cotton thread from his clothing.

He had also stolen some notepaper which he sewed, with a needle made from wood, into two small books. One became a German-Russian dictionary, the other a recipe book. Remlinger's inventiveness was so sophisticated that he crocheted a cosy for his tin mug. Thomsen emulated much that Remlinger did and went one better—he made a Danish-English-German-Russian dictionary. Thomsen, a doctor, also passed a lot of time in designing hospitals and evolving administrative systems for them. He became so engrossed while at Butirka that he did not even hear the shrieks of tortured prisoners.

Many prisoners have made chessmen from bread and Rupert, in Camp 10, Russia, made a pipe from dough. When dried in an oven it was quite usable and did not burn away. Phallic symbols, tiny ornamental weapons, whole model villages, and all manner of personal objects inspired by nostalgia and homesickness are made from dough.

Unable to eat the boiled potatoes or the semolina boiled in water, Edith Bone "started a flourishing bookbinding workshop and patience card factory", using the boiled semolina as paste and her own weight as a press.

The captive who indulges in the satisfaction of such creativity runs great risks, for after months of industry he might find his whole collection wantonly destroyed or confiscated by a guard. Great will is then needed to start again.

Less satisfying than physical creativity but generally safer is physical activity, of which the most obvious example is exercise. Mrs. de Beausobre and the four women in her cell decided on regular exercise, not so much because it would "do them good" as for something to do. Zoia, a natural acrobat, could easily walk the length of the cell and back on her hands; Mrs. de Beausobre had only one ability, to support all her weight on her shoulders and the nape of her neck while she moved her legs in various ways. Natalia knew many amusing breathing exercises. Out of their store of knowledge the women made up a series of exercises and performed them systematically every morning before being taken to the washroom.

In a crowded cell an exercise roster system is necessary. If six men occupy a small cell, five must crouch against the walls while the sixth takes four steps forward and four back. No momentum can be built up, so about twenty-five minutes are needed to walk a mile. In winter, endless walking must be interrupted more and more frequently by intervals of sitting or lying tightly wrapped in the blankets. After a lot of practice in concentrated immobility, a man can will himself into near-anaesthesia for perhaps an hour at a time, a form of time-filling in itself.

Father Ciszek spent much time polishing his cell floor and mending his clothes, using needles made from fish bones. He spent at least forty-five minutes daily in physical exercises.

Another prison activity in groups is fortune-telling, a dangerous game to play, for the "fortune" told can be too unpleasantly close to reality and to the client's fears. Still, among experienced captives it can be diverting, if they have a sense of humour. "You have friends working for your release and you will be out of prison in three weeks," the day's seer may say. Or, "You can expect extra food tomorrow." A special analysis could cost as much as half a day's bread ration, but men will pay this stiff price for the chance of hearing hopeful news. Many convince themselves that a prediction is correct and are bitterly disappointed when it is not.

General Emilian Ionescu, while a prisoner in Jilava, invented a system of fortune-telling with cards which became immensely popular. He would deal out four poker hands—for freedom, delay, trial, and removal from the present cell. The better the hand, the better the chance of the particular thing happening. A refinement was specific results from specific cards, so that, for example, four aces meant immediate freedom.

Gambling, for imaginary stakes or for food, is a common group activity and can lead to dangerous enmities. The prisoner who loses his small food ration immediately hates the winner; the hatred becomes so deep that he may even attempt to murder his "enemy". Some prisoners lose all sense of property. Popoff nearly lost his boots in a dice game; he himself was not a player, but a tougher comrade used Popoff's boots as a stake. Popoff would probably have surrendered them, but another cell-mate stood up for him.

Koestler scrawled mathematical formulae on his cell wall, working out the equation for an ellipse, among other things. But tolerant guards are needed for wall-work since it is an offence in most prisons to deface cell walls.

Other captives spend much time knocking on walls in the hope of being able to strike up a vicarious friendship by means of the "prisoner's alphabet", a type of cipher which enables conversations

161

to be held. Such contact is easier if the cells have plumbing, as sounds travel freely along pipes. It is possible to speak directly into a toilet bowl and have the words heard clearly in some other cell. Kazinczy, "father of Hungarian letters", was happy enough to use the prisoner's alphabet in the dungeons of Kufstein while in prison for involvement in the Jacobin conspiracy at the end of the eighteenth century.

In Buchenwald and Dachau, Bettelheim found the favourite free time group activity was "exchanging tales of woe and swapping rumours", generally about changes in camp conditions. He also knew two prisoners whose deep interest in stamp collecting drew them together and gave them something to talk about in captivity. But this safety valve refused to function after a time because the two men had nothing new to feed into their association. Bettelheim saw their friendship turn sour as the men became morose and beaten.

Preoccupation with pets can also be considered a physical activity. A bird brought some joy into the life of Byron's "prisoner of Chillon", but much less poetic creatures have brightened existence for other captives. In his cell in Venice, Pellico made pets of the ants that infested his window-sill and fed them so well with crumbs of food that other ants came, much to his satisfaction. He enjoyed the company of a spider which had a web on one of the walls and fed it flies and mosquitoes; patiently he trained it to crawl all the way to his bed to take food from his fingers. He also made a pet of a deaf-mute about six years old, the orphaned child of executed parents. He did not know the child's name, but the companionship of this little thing, for whom he developed a paternal love, gave him infinite satisfaction.

Koestler was visited by a small black cat which sat on his window ledge; he was upset that the wire grille prevented him from stroking the animal, for he desperately wanted its company.

Burney, on a rare occasion when he was allowed out for exercise, picked a snail off the wall and took it back to his cell for company. In isolation at Baden, near Vienna, Rupert found "strange satisfaction" in observing spiders spinning, and watched fascinated as flies flew into the webs, where the spiders first stung and then ravaged their victims. A mouse and its family gave him more satisfaction. They brought him a "whole new world" and he managed to keep so still that the mice played in front of him and would eat the breadcrumbs he gave them.

In Jilava, Kirschen speaks of having crickets, bats and mice as pets. There was at least one dog, which was popular with the prisoners until the guards did away with him. Even catching bugs and fleas becomes an absorbing pastime when there is nothing else to do. Begin says, "Only the first louse will move you to ask fearfully: 'To what have I been brought?' As their numbers increase you will fight them; they will win. You will get used to them. They will get used to you. You will live with them; and you will want to live, even with them."

All physical occupations have their limits and limitations, but the imagination and the intellect are not so bounded and can be profitably used for time-filling. Sir Walter Raleigh, at the age of fifty-one, was imprisoned in the Tower of London for alleged treason and spent thirteen years there. He wrote essays on current political problems, political philosophy, on ships and war by sea and lengthy historical works. The *History of the World* fills six large volumes. Raleigh was prematurely old, sick, despairing, and preoccupied with schemes for release, and that he could finish such a work says much for his determination.

Short of paper, Pellico wrote letters, poems, philosophy and much else on his table top, and when it was covered would scrape it clean and begin again. He wrote a poem on Christopher Columbus and another on the Lombard League, as well as the outlines of several plays. He induced the young daughter of one of his warders to make him coffee so strong that it mildly intoxicated him and stimulated him into wakefulness all night. During these periods he not only wrote inspired poetry, but was capable of impassioned philosophy and prayer.

A group of intelligent and educated prisoners in the one cell is sometimes better off than a lone prisoner. After the first demoralising shock of captivity most such men can organise their time; some have systematic courses of instruction—history, languages, archaeology, ethics, literature and so on. When Paloczi-Horvath was in Vác Prison, he and five cell-mates had a lecture course on world history, with each man speaking on the period he knew best. A well integrated group of considerate men can perhaps live peacefully for a month under these conditions, but after that quarrels occur.

Nerves are taut, frustration acute, there are no distractions and men become hypersensitive. A simple statement or action is readily misinterpreted. Some captives collapse frequently.

In Lubianka between 1941 and 1945, Father Ciszek spent the mornings in reciting prayers and hymns. In the afternoon he would recite poetry, such as Wordsworth's "We are Seven", Shelley's "Ode to the West Wind" and Burns' poem to a field mouse. Also, pretending to be Stalin, he would ask himself silly questions and take delight in answering in a silly way. When he was allowed books he read nearly all of Tolstoy's work, then devoured Dostoievski, Turgenev, Gogol, Leskov, Lenin, Jack London, Dickens, Shakespeare, Goethe, Schiller, all in Russian.* He so schooled himself to reading that he completed one book a day. This was satisfying, but he had so little contact with other people that he became almost tongue-tied in talking with the doctor or warden on their infrequent visits.

In Camp 14, to which Rupert was sent in the early 1950s, the lingua franca was English. A Lithuanian poet, Nishkinis, though he had never been to England, spoke excellent English and gave a series of prison lectures on Byron and Keats, though he risked punishment if caught. Another prisoner, a former Bucharest correspondent of the *Daily Mail*, dredged into his astonishing memory and wrote out on rough packing paper extracts from English novels and short stories.

Burney each morning would sit on his stool and order himself not to stand until he had listed all the counties of the British Isles and the states and capitals of the United States. A further mental and physical exercise was to sit, pupil-like, and make journeys from one place to another, naming the towns and peoples on the way and listing their languages and trades.

In Vác Prison in 1954, Edith Bone decided to study mathematics and demanded a pair of compasses, a protractor, a slide-rule, a ruler and graph paper, as well as a book of logarithms and angular function tables. Obtaining these, she "revelled" in trigonometry, quadratic equations, and co-ordinate geometry. She read Thackeray's

* In Russian prisons, studying English is forbidden, although when the cold war war began to thaw after Stalin's death there was some relaxation of this rule. Russian itself cannot be studied by non-Russians because it could help prisoners attempting to escape. After the thaw, sports, concerts and film shows were organised and it became lawful for prisoners to form cultural groups and to attend lectures on almost any subject.

Pendennis, and also *Nicholas Nickleby*. Another of her intellectual exercises was to remember characters from fiction; she was able to remember 400 from Dickens alone.

In a dark cell for five months Edith Bone translated poems from one language to another—she knew six languages. She drew some solace from her memories of Silvio Pellico's book and from other prison literature. Ignotus too read Pellico's memoirs with "wistful delight". Myrna Blumberg found some solace in reflecting on Tolstoy's *The Resurrection* and on Edith Bone's book on her seven years' solitary confinement.

In Roeland Street Gaol in Cape Town, Miss Blumberg and her eight cell-mates discoursed and lectured on a greater range of subjects than any male political prisoner has been able to record. However, in another respect they could not equal men. The Blumberg group tried to organise "silent hours" at eleven a.m. and three p.m., but this merely reduced talking aloud to frustrated and irritated whispering. Groups of men are able to remain in complete silence for hours at a time.

A frequent pastime in solitary, at least among the more dispassionate and objective prisoners, is to pass judgment on past behaviour. Paloczi-Horvath found, however, "that this might be a more praiseworthy pastime for people wiser and safer" than himself. Judging one's actions involves an assessment of character and personality, in itself an absorbing pastime, in which a man comes face to face with the truth whether he likes it or not. He realises that he is a bundle of illusions, influenced by his own time and his own place. In prison, both timeless and placeless after a relatively short period in solitary, he may see his basic nature more clearly. But many prisoners are unable to face the breaking down of their illusions under prison conditions.

Most politicals who have undergone solitary have evolved similar systems in an effort to find fuel for the mind. With nothing new to hear or see or read, they have had to fall back on memory. To most people a book read years before is merely a blur in the memory. An intelligent captive, alone for endless hours, patiently dredges up more and more details and can see, after a while, whole paragraphs of the book. With this sort of exercise the mental muscles seem to improve, but a great effort is generally needed to make the initial effort to *want* to think. Some politicals report dividing the days into distinct periods of mental activity; in one a man may lecture himself, in another he translates a passage from one language to another, yet again he may play a mental game of chess with an imaginary opponent.

The imagination, as distinct from disciplined intellectual thought, has given many prisoners hours of time-occupation. At one time, in Seville, Koestler amused himself by inventing "a peripatetic dialogue" between Karl Marx and Sigmund Freud on the causes of the Great War.

One of the most pleasurable but at the same time most distressing of imagination experiences is to think about girls, lingering over their features and their figures and their delights. If carried too far this can lead to masturbation or nocturnal emission.

It is possible, too, to be another person—to live the life of a Cromwellian Roundhead, as Paloczi-Horvath did, or that of a Spanish adventurer or even a Hollywood mogul with the money to indulge every sensuous and artistic taste.

Frankl, a trained and experienced psychiatrist, rose above his sufferings of the moment by vividly imagining that he was standing on the platform of an expensive lecture room giving a talk about the psychology of the concentration camp. He took mental bus rides to his apartment, where he answered telephone calls and switched on electric lights.

For most men the most dangerous time comes in the evenings when they are tired but are prevented by gaol rules from lying down to sleep. It was in the evenings that Paloczi-Horvath permitted himself the luxury of reliving his travels; as he had travelled in forty countries he had plenty of material. One of these mental trips involved a journey from Cairo to Istanbul, which he had made eleven times during World War II. The journey took five days but when the captive first relived it it lasted only two hours; he knew the period exactly because of prison routine. Later he made a second mental trip, remembering much more, and did not finish the trip in an entire evening. When he made the trip a third time, towards the end of his time in solitary, he was still travelling after three entire evenings. Details were startlingly clear; he even saw the faces of several sleeping-car attendants on trains and those of fellow-passengers, and could relive his changing moods of the journey.

Like Paloczi-Horvath, Edith Bone made mental trips. She walked observantly around cities from London to Heidelberg, Vienna to Florence; she hiked from Budapest to the English Channel four times and often called on friends.

It is rare for boredom to drive a prisoner to extreme lengths of compensation and rarer still for him to find an opportunity to carry out elaborate plans. One of the few such stories concerns a prisoner, an actor in normal life, serving a long sentence at Norilsk in Siberia. One of a party detailed to move the furniture and belongings of an MVD general, the prisoner stole one of the general's uniforms, and later, dressed in it, he walked out of the prison. It would have been impossible for him to leave Siberia, so he contented himself with an elaborate hoax. He travelled to Dudinka, a notorious prison settlement, where he arrived "to make a thorough inspection". He reprimanded and cursed officials of every rank, ordered food and clothing to be distributed and insisted on many improvements. He confiscated all the account books and cash boxes "for a more detailed examination" and took them away with him. Finally, at a full parade, he castigated the staff in front of the prisoners. By the time the alarm had been sounded about a missing uniform and a missing prisoner, he was back in Norilsk. According to one report he was never discovered.

Not one of these four usual methods of time-filling is adequate in itself, and the captive who best adjusts to prison life uses all methods. Without the trivia which make up much of a day in normal life, twenty-four hours is a long period. Just as the prisoner's body in time consumes its own protein, the brain seems to consume itself, and in prolonged captivity the stage is reached when everything has been done and thought so many times that only a mere existence remains.

10
Religion

○○○○○○

Religion among political prisoners provides some strange conflicts and most men are, at one time or another during their captivity, torn between faith and disillusionment. It might be expected that many, after years of frightful privations and complete loss of hope, would be ready to deny the existence of any god. It might with equal reason be argued that in the extremities of political captivity they would naturally turn to a god as a last resort. Probably the actual position is a compromise between the two, though it must be said that among those captives who have left memoirs and letters, the majority clearly show a definite belief and faith in God, though many had little faith when first imprisoned. In his prison camps, Frankl found prisoners' religious interest the "most sincere imaginable". Prisoner-priests, of whom there have been many, have often been responsible, by their own fine example, for this sincerity.

However, Burney thought that belief in doctrine was easy, and that listening to it was agreeable "as long as the Sunday beef was sizzling in the oven". But under the stress of the test he faced he found the Bible's words barren. He had come near to believing in God at one point, but after being beaten up and then coming back to his cell and an evil-smelling bowl of stale cabbage soup, he could not hold to his near-belief. Rather did he remember, and tend to agree with, what somebody has said of the New Testament: "It is the finest known piece of propaganda because it tells people exactly what they want to hear."

But Begin says that prison persecution at the hands of the Russians "brought many prisoners back to the religious fold". Kirschen's great fear that he would never be released and that he would die in gaol turned him to God. The only prayer he knew was the Lord's Prayer in English, but he was unable to concentrate on it and fell back on original prayer, mostly pleas that he be saved from insanity and fear.

After eight months of isolation and interrogation in Baden (Vienna) prison, Rupert collapsed and spent ten days in an hallucinatory coma, during which he saw the head of Christ, the head and shoulders of a Franciscan monk offering him a cross, and a flying angel. By the time he reached a Russian prison, more than a year after his arrest, Rupert was convinced that the only way he could withstand suffering would be to "put himself into the hands of God".

Sylvia Salvesen, the wife of a Norwegian professor, wrote in an illicit letter to friends, "I can only thank God for these years in prison, for I realise that during this time He has given me a definite message, and I thank God also for the comrades whom, thanks to my faith, my age and my position here in hospital, I have been allowed to help."

Heimler prayed to his mother for help and became extremely close to her; her nearness was a major factor in bringing him through his ordeal, while Julius Leber, a prisoner of the Nazis, wrote, "I have been turning over many thoughts in the last few weeks, and I have at all events reached the conviction that the love of which the soul of man is capable, and which is stronger than anything else in man or in the world, shows that this soul must be of divine origin. And to be of divine origin means also to be immortal."

Thomsen both prayed to God and cursed Him during his early days in captivity, but later he acquired "an inner strength . . . a wonderful sense of certainty . . . call it God".

It must be remembered that in most periods and in most political prisons authority has refused to countenance religion; this, in itself, is an inducement to many captives to make use of it, according to the simple law that what is forbidden is attractive. However, it may also be argued that since interest in religion can lead to punishment, men's interest in it must be, in part, genuine. There is no doubt that Lance's faith was pure. In a Valencia prison in 1937, he found his prayer book a tremendous source of strength and inspiration, and belief in God his only salvation. Having preserved his illicit prayer book for months, Lance had it seized during a routine search in a gaol in Barcelona. The guard who uncovered it kicked Lance, swore foully at him, blasphemed furiously and ground the prayer book to pieces with his boot. Authority at a higher level punished Lance by parading him through the streets of Barcelona in an open truck, while the street mobs shouted insults at him. The culmination of his punishment came at a splendid chapel, where Lance was forced to destroy the altar with a crowbar.

A Norwegian, Petter Moen, left some interesting letters about his religious thoughts. A lawyer, he was arrested on February 4, 1944, and after seven months in prison was deported to Germany with 400 others. In Skagerrak, the prisoners' transport struck a mine and Petter Moen lost his life with the rest. Statements made by one of the few survivors led to the discovery of his diary under the floor of his cell in the Oslo prison, in the form of hundreds of rolls of paper with a barely legible script of pin pricks. He wrote:

. . . I fear there will be mass executions. May a higher power defend us. On my knees I have prayed to the God of my father and mother, I prayed for my life and for the lives of my comrades. I weep a great deal. I am not brave. I am no hero. There is nothing I can do about it. I am only abysmally unhappy.

. . . Is my "desire for God" honest? It could be an *argumentum ad hoc*—a product of imprisonment. It has been said that belief in God is a creation of fear—the fear of nature and the fear of death. If that is the case, then I am on the right road. I believe that I can "find God" through suffering, fear, and prayer. Then have I played a trick on myself? Has spiritual exercise mastered my intellect? I cannot answer this question now, I only know that suffering and fear are terrible realities and that in the hour of suffering and fear I call out: Help me, God! This cry helps me. It stills the fear and occasionally keeps it away from me. Is it to be said, then, that God has helped?

Lehndorff-Steinort, an officer condemned to death for his part in the attempt to kill Hitler and overthrow the Nazi regime on July 20, 1944, wrote on the eve of his execution:

170

My disposition . . . and above all, the help of God for which I have always besought Him and which He has given me freely, have allowed me to overcome all trials in a way that I would never have thought possible. A total transformation is taking place . . . I could not explain better than by means of the saying from the Bible, "Be not afraid, only believe".

The main contribution of the Dutch resistance consisted in rescue work and in the protection of individuals persecuted by the Nazis. Many thousands lost their lives in this service. In commemoration of the liberation of Holland, the Dutch newspaper *In de Waagschaal* published the last letter of one of the members of the resistance, Harmen van der Leek, executed in November, 1941. In 1951 the letter was republished in the German monthly *Die Neue Furche,* but no further information about the writer is available. It is worth quoting not only for the writer's comments on religion but to show the devastating effects of uncertainty.

Beloved Pastor and Friend: What an experience we have had again! On Friday four of us were first taken to Amsterdam by car, and we were in very high spirits. One of us had been told that we were to have another hearing, and, since the death sentence had already been pronounced this could have meant a favourable turn of events. But the blow that came after was all the harder.

We still had three hours to live, and we could write our last letters. I did that and then waited for your arrival. I spoke to Pastor Ferwerda for a moment and was able to assure him that all was well with me. There was nothing else that I could say, for I was infinitely calm and full of courage. How could I otherwise have been so gay? I was able to take leave of everyone and everything—and with that the last tie that still bound me to earth was severed. But then, a quarter of an hour before the scheduled time, came the report—postponement. That completely crushed me. With death before my eyes, I was never for a moment troubled: my trust in God remained strong. When I was shut up in the terrible, heavily barred death cell, I even had an impulse for an instant to sing out loud. I looked at all the iron with a smile. And then when the door was locked behind me, I thought: Now the door of life is closing for ever for me. But immediately the thought came to me clearly and firmly: If God so wills, he can still free me, even from this place. But I had not the slightest feeling of hurt or disappointment, not the slightest desire that He do so.

However, to be flung from the certainty of death back into fear and doubt and new anticipation made me inwardly weak. Of course I remained certain of God's infinite goodness in Jesus Christ, and certain that He knows better than I; yet I had to implore His special help, screaming and sobbing, to be able to bear this new shock. For two days I, together with my cell-mates, suffered under it; at times we were able to speak with one another about God's great mercy, but the certainty that I should be saved was gone. This did not cause me to revolt against God—in the first sleepless night between Friday and Saturday I fought the last fight and learned anew to pray, "Thy will be done". I said: "Lord, I am finished. Here you have me, completely, impotent and beaten. Now I await nothing more but your mercy."

But my faith was not shattered. I came only to this conclusion, that God's plan for me in relation to this time or to eternity was not yet completed. During the night I awoke and felt that my whole faith had returned. I still feel pain and fear, for now I know what probably lies before me; but this also serves to calm me, for it is no longer unexpected. However, I am certain that even in this God will help us through. We are now prepared for the end. At the same time, I still possess my full belief in God's miraculous power; even now He can still save us and bless the last efforts that are being made for us in Berlin. But I feel that I no longer want to grasp at this possibility; I only want to wait quietly, like a child, for my Father's decision. I must suffer, but not as one who is without hope. Whatever comes will be good, even of unexpected splendour. We pray that we may be allowed to live as powerful witnesses for the Saviour; more than that we do not ask. As you see, a clear, unalloyed attitude is not within my capacity, but I wait for the Lord . . .

Pellico speaks of "the blessing of prayer". At times he remained for several hours "with my mind raised to God" and his trust in God increased. It was only through prayer that he could regain peace of mind after being upset by some unpleasant happening in prison. Pellico prayed constantly and sincerely, but not from the sheer self pity which inspires the prayers of some prisoners. He found that "the joy of living" could be felt even in the midst of prison miseries "by one who considers that God is present". As a matter of principle he tried not to complain about anything, though he found solitude almost unbearable, despite the advantage of having a copy of the Bible and of Dante; he learnt a canto of Dante by heart every day, and the Bible, which he had always liked, he appreciated more deeply than before.

Pellico even managed to rationalise his suffering by convincing himself that he deserved to be punished by God—though he is never very clear in his writings what sins he had committed that merited such severe punishment. One of his recent biographers, a priest, saw Pellico as "utterly purified of dross" during his captivity. But this is a little too poetic to be true. At the time of his sentencing to fifteen years in Spielberg, he did give way to hate. It was a pleasure more attractive than forgiving, he said. In his distress "the universe seemed the work of a power opposed to good".

In the end, though, it was in prison that he finally decided to draw the conclusion: love God and your neighbour. Count Antonio Oroboni, a prisoner in the Spielberg when Pellico was there, was another who forgave his enemies while actually in prison. His Christian charity was so deep and sincere that even Pellico felt humble in the face of it. He died in the Spielberg; his last words, as reported by Pellico, were, "From my heart I forgive my enemies."

"Prison," wrote Pellico, "is like the world, in that those who think it wisdom to rage, to complain, to scorn others, hold it folly to have sympathy, to love, to find consolation in thoughts that honour humanity and its Author." Pellico came into contact with men made bitter by prison life; they simply could not understand him when he preached hope and brotherly love and told them of the little things that gave tenderness even to prison life.

One of the most outstanding religious groups in prison are Jehovah's Witnesses, who have won the often reluctant admiration and respect of other prisoners and even of gaolers. In Ravensbruck, Sylvia Salvesen found the Witnesses' strength, endurance, peace and joy incredible. Other observers say that the Witnesses were rarely troubled or worried about themselves, but that their hymn-singing and Bible-reading sometimes irritated others. The two Bibles given to Mrs. Salvesen by the Witnesses in Ravensbruck

173

helped her, more than anything else, to endure her twenty-two months in Nazi captivity.

Possibly the most revealing effects of religion in prison are shown by the attitudes of priests, since they more than others find their theological theory put to extreme tests. In Russia, Nazi Germany and Hungary particularly, priest-prisoners have been more savagely treated and disgustingly humiliated than other men. St. Paul, himself a political prisoner, wrote: "I have learned, in whatever state I am, therein to be content. I know how to be abused, and I also know how to abound . . . I can do all things in Him that strengtheneth me . . . "

Much slanderous and ill-informed comment has been made about prisoner-priests in Nazi concentration camps, perhaps because the priests had to be secretive about most of their actions. Many of them died for their beliefs. When typhus epidemics broke out in prison hospitals the priests were the only ones who would nurse the sick; many of the priest-nurses died of typhus.

Rupert reports that priest-prisoners were outstanding for the work they did in the gaols of Russia. "Their wisdom and philosophical calm in the midst of so much unhappiness and suffering gave us the necessary courage and spiritual force to go on."

Judaism affects political prisoners differently from other religions. Few Jewish prisoners have acknowledged that their religious faith helped them to bear their captivity and, as a religious group—rather than an ethnic one—they appear oddly disunited in prison. This could be due to there being such vast numbers of Jews in prison during the Nazi regime; minority religious groups probably tend to be more united, militant and vocal. Émile Mercier, a French Jew who endured eight years of captivity, says,* "I cannot recall having had a single religious thought or in any way having leant on my faith. This is true of my immediate friends in prison. For us religion was an aspect of normal life. It was rare for a rabbi to survive even long enough to reach a prison and I never met one, but it was possible to meet priests of other creeds. Had it been possible for Jewish prisoners to centre some sort of religious life on professional spiritual leaders they could perhaps have displayed more fervour. But leadership simply did not exist."

Nor does much written evidence exist of Judaism in prison. In

* In a letter to the author.

1937 Paul Hintz, pastor of the Cathedral of St. Mary at Kolberg, published a collection of letters and other documents written in Nazi prisons by clergymen of various denominations but he was unable to find any reference to Judaism. Similarly, in 1956 the editors of *Dying We Live*, a record of prisoners' "last letters", failed to uncover anything from a Jewish source. All this is significant.

A Jew, Elias Heyor, who became a rabbi in the United States after several years as a political prisoner, wrote in 1949,* that Jewish prisoners had a "consciousness of faith" without a conscious need to use it as did men of other religions. "We were persecuted not because of our politics but because we were Jews by birth. Yet our nationality and our religion are indivisible and because of this attack on our very being our religion was driven into a state of suspended animation." He implies that since other men were persecuted primarily because of their politics they were much freer to practice their religion, which was a secondary "offence" in the eyes of their captors.

This appears to be borne out by the relative freedom of Jews in Russian prison camps to engage in some religious practice, though the urge to do so seems rare. On occasions when men of varied religions have held combined services the Jews have rarely taken advantage of the opportunity. This is not because they are irreligious or unreligious. Mercier crystallises the Jewish attitude by insisting that "Judaism under captivity becomes an intellectual faith, while that of, say, Roman Catholics, is an emotional faith. Hence it is entirely inward but it was no less strong in prison for being invisible."

Rejecting any belief which is not compatible with reason, Judaism demands blind faith only in the existence of God, since this is not demonstrable by reason. Yet, concerned with far more than an abstract series of beliefs and injunctions, Judaism is something very much more than a religion. The connection between Judaism and the Jewish people has been one of the most potent factors in the survival of both. This complete bond had a great effect on the emergence of Zionism and on the ultimate establishment of the State of Israel. A religion so strong was certainly alive in political prisoners, though it may not be discussed and may not even be thought of consciously.

* In *Atlantic Monthly*.

Enemies of the Jews have rarely understood anything of their religion. A leading Nazi writer, Alfred Rosenberg, wrote in 1937,* "It is impossible for a genuine German to accept a God of the Jews . . . " To most anti-Semites the word "Jew" merely implies a race or sub-race of people, a way of life, a political outlook or even an economic philosophy, with religion as a minor characteristic.

Evangelist prisoners, in contrast to the Jews, have been few, but they too have been remarkably well armoured by their faith. Typical of them was Pastor Ludwig Steil, of Holsterhausen, Germany, who in November 1944 wrote to his daughter from prison, "Your father is being reminded once more that he must learn anew, as a prisoner, to maintain a cheerful heart and to say to the good Lord, 'Hence I wait patiently, Thy word holds no deceit. Thou knowst the way for me: That doth suffice'."

Writing to other Evangelist pastors, Steil urged that as they followed the way of the confessional church, they were not to contemplate the failures of man but must contemplate God's miracles. It is characteristic of Evangelists in their letters and writings which survive never to refer to their enemies, even indirectly. They might not have existed. Steil and others were concerned mainly with keeping up the spirits of their families and fellow believers and they rarely gave way to self interest, let alone self pity.

The nearest Steil comes to introspection is an admission, again in November 1944, that he lay awake for an hour one night and put many questions to God. "They were posed not in the spirit of challenge but only out of longing for an answer. And suddenly the verses of a long-forgotten hymn sung in East Berlin rang in my ears and silenced me, 'Oh, that thou could'st believe, then would'st thou wonders see, for by thy side for evermore, thy Saviour then would be'."

As he waited for execution in January 1945 Steil was composed enough to ask in his only letter from Dachau, "Where will God's way lead us now? But he himself always stands at the end of the road. That restores us."

Major research could profitably be carried out on the use political captives have made of their religion. A comparative study, though leading to invidious conclusions, could also be interesting. But much

* *Heroisimus und Weltangst*, 1937.

176

data would need to be collected. A few priests fail the test, but the vast majority do not succumb to the doctrine of survival at any cost and carry out their religious duties with extraordinary courage and dedication. One such man was Karl Leisner, who was afflicted in his early days in prison at Freiberg with endless and intense self-interrogation. One of the most vital questions was, "Am I really guilty of some crime in the eyes of God and is this why I am here?" But like more mundane men he had his share of the usual self-questions: "Why in the name of reason am I here?" or "How can I possibly prove my innocence?" He prayed, but his prayers seemed to be unanswered. Then renewed efforts brought forth a sort of pure prayer which seemed to bear results in practical and spiritual ways. But even prayer could not gain him a release and for reasons of "public security" he was sent to Sachsenhausen concentration camp.

Only twenty-six when he was gaoled in Dachau, Leisner had a tremendous struggle with himself to achieve a state of mind that would enable him to be some help to his fellow prisoners. In addition, he had a serious pulmonary disease which was aggravated by prison conditions. A comrade in captivity, Otto Pies, says that Leisner suffered terribly from the "vulgarity, injustice, slavery and utter degradation", but he was probably the only man in Dachau who never had a personal enemy; even the SS guards treated him with relative humanity.

In Dachau, from the beginning of 1941, about 850 priests,* rounded up from several other prison camps, were considered so dangerous that they were isolated within the prison itself, so that they should have no contact with the other captives. The SS and many of the other prisoners themselves were in agreement that the priests were a threat. The many prisoners whose one concern was survival at any and all costs feared that the priests would preach self sacrifice. Many other captives had already developed some kind of inner resistance to the horror of their life and did not want it disturbed by religion.

Karl Leisner was ordained in Dachau prison late in 1944. The

* The priests in Dachau represented twenty-five nations and forty religious orders; the Jesuits, with ninety-five prisoners, were the most prominent. Their ages ranged from 82, a Lithuanian pastor, to 18, theology students.

service, carried out with all ceremony and performed by Bishop Gabriel Piquet of Clermont-Ferrand, another prisoner, was a masterpiece of secrecy. Yet it lacked nothing of the customary trappings—including red shoes, mitre, ring and staff for the bishop, all made in the prison. The organisers even managed to obtain permission from the Archbishop of Munich, via their permanent underground link with the outside. One hundred prisoners attended the ordination—unique in the history of political captivity. Father Karl wore his white alb over his prison clothes, carrying his folded priestly vestments over his left arm and a burning candle in his right hand. He died from illness soon after the war ended.

A Jesuit, Alfred Delp, who was to be executed by hanging, wrote on November 30, 1944:

> Today is another very black day. God must really be very intensively concerned with me, in that he has thrown me so exclusively on my own resources. For some time now I have again been totally isolated. I am to learn what faith and trust mean . . . Sometimes I tell the Lord God that I need a bit of consoling . . . Sometimes I also ask for a word of guidance and consolation, and open the Scriptures at random. Just now I opened to "Those who believe will work the following miracles", etc . . . I made the "play" once more and this time I opened to Matthew, Chapter 20, again a word of assurance.

Father Rupert Mayer, a Jesuit born in 1876, resisted the National Socialist enemies of the Christian faith with inflexible courage. Scornful of compromise, he refused to belong to what was termed "underground" Germany. From the outset he defended himself in words: "It seems much more honest to me clearly to state what is afoot than to wind through a maze of phraseology. When I speak, people know where I stand and that I shall not budge." In prison he, too, found consolation:

> I have now passed through the most beautiful period of my life. One would not believe that possible. I have been happy, completely happy, as I have never before been in my life. In the course of these weeks the dear Lord has let me know—and I am a man of reason—that he is satisfied with me. That makes me happy; all else cannot disturb me. Prison is better for me than a thousand lectures on behalf of the Catholic community, on apologetics, on the Gospel—much better than if I were to

lecture on heaven knows what . . . After a life rich in rewards,
but also rich in disappointments and ingratitude, I have now
landed happily in prison. But I am in no way dissatisfied with
this lot. I consider it not a disgrace, but rather the crowning of
life . . . How easy God can make things, through His own
omnipotent grace, for those who must, or, better, are allowed
to die for our holy faith.

Being generally articulate men, priests have left many letters
concerning their stay in political prisons; the few I have quoted are
representative. It is possible to see in them not only faith, but a
balanced mind and a sense of humour. But the strongest and most
consistent note is one of acceptance of the situation, almost as if it
were theologically viable.

Sometimes a priest visits a gaol not as a prisoner but as a chaplain.
Not all captives have been glad of this though comparatively few
have admitted as much in their writings. One explanation of their
attitude must be that men most want a priest when they know they
are about to die and they are apt to acknowledge God when in this
extremity. Short of this point they are not so ready to accept a visit
from the chaplain. Some political prisoners have admitted that they
have been curt, even rude, to a priest in prison. This happens for
one of several reasons. Some captives, suspiciously sensitive, fear
that the priest may be sent to gain their confidence so as to spy on
them; some resent the priest's ability to come and go as he pleases;
others have lost all religious faith and are affronted by what one
prisoner calls "holy hypocrisy", others still have no use for a God
that performs the double function of saviour and scourge.

Burney tells of the title, from a psalm, of a sermon left by a
chaplain in a prisoner's cell: "For all our days are passed away in
Thy wrath; we spend our years as a tale that is told". Burney says
this second phrase, "Must be the best description ever given of a
prisoner's life."

We have noted elsewhere that unity and camaraderie are generally
unknown among political prisoners, so it is striking to find one
experienced witness, Rupert, who suggests that at least captives
are united in the essentials of a common hope and faith. Towards the
end of his imprisonment in Russia in 1954, Rupert attended a prison
church service in which Protestants, Roman Catholics, Baptists,
Uniats, Buddhists, Jews. Jehovah's Witnesses, Armenian Indepen-

dent Free Catholics and even Mohammedans sang the Te Deum together.

This analysis of religion among politicals is not meant to leave the impression that belief, trust and faith in God is a paramount force in prison. It is for some men in some circumstances, for many men during brief intervals. Much depends on religious upbringing and teaching; much more depends, as Burney so soberly says, on the Sunday beef. When a man is really and truly hungry there can be no real and true religion beyond the preaching of his empty belly.

11

Sex

○○○

Sex in a prison full of political captives is not the searing problem that a casual inquirer might assume it to be. This statement needs much qualification but as a generalisation it is true. Under the normal prison conditions of extreme hunger, cold, anxiety and loss of personality and dignity even the most virile of men will, after a time, lose all desire during waking hours, though it lives on in his dreams. Those captives who have survived to write their recollections have little to say about sex in any of its aspects. One prisoner, Schiller,* says, "I was an ardent man with an intense need for normal sexual relations. For the first month in prison I hardly had a sexual thought or impulse, all being driven out of my system by fear and apprehension. For the following two months desire recurred and I suffered deeply and masturbated frequently. After that desire rapidly ran down and virtually disappeared. I used to try deliberately to rouse myself by imagining myself in the most provocative situations, but nothing happened. Twelve months later I had a single nocturnal emission. It was the only sexual manifestation in five years."

Prisoners' experiences differ so much that Schiller's cannot be taken as typical. Still, the idea that men under these conditions became raving mad from sexual repression and frustration is misconceived. As Christopher Burney found, "sex goes to sleep". And

* In a letter to the author. He is speaking of the period 1950-55 in Hungary.

181

his conditions, though severe, were not as arduous as those suffered by many other captives.

There has probably never been a normal prisoner who has not feared for his sexual potency, and many are inclined to prove it by masturbation or homosexuality. However, few men did this very often and, as Bettelheim points out, it was more for proof of potency than for enjoyment. After a time in prison, when poor food and great anxiety have had their effect, the prisoner is concerned with conserving his strength and not dissipating it in masturbation. Understandably, most men who have endured solitary for a long period and lived to write about it have not disclosed whether they masturbated, but psychologists say that when they do so it is partly engendered by self pity, partly from boredom, and only little from sexual repression.

Many a prisoner has been convinced of his impotence only to find on release that he had been suffering from malnutrition and lassi-tude.* In the end, most prisoners sublimate and satisfy their sex urges through their dreams.

Many prisoners seem to agree that the older a captive is the less he misses his wife; her importance to him decreases with the years. This is not a unanimous view but it seems clear that the younger men missed their wives more physically than in any other way, while the older men needed companionship. Younger men suffer torments from sexual longings. It is not that they are necessarily innately passionate or sex-conscious. But a man in a man's world thinks and talks about women not only for the sexual union they represent, but for the softer side of life they symbolise. The pheno-menon is as widely known in armies as in gaol populations. The two sides of female appeal become confused and more intense, so intense that young men, while still reasonably fed and in good health, throw themselves at their cell walls in the frenzy of their repressions and desires.

Some long term captives—A.D. was one—have tried to find an inner freedom from sexual need. They take the view, or try to do so, that the real problems of existence begin with complete control of the imagination by moral and intellectual means.

Other men resort to homosexuality but among politicals this seems

*For an account of the post-prison sexual difficulties of prisoners see *Children of Auschwitz*, an essay by Eugene Heimler, in *Prison*.

rare, partly because captives are too weak for such diversion, even
more because such activity with a large audience at close range
would require a peculiar sort of temperament on the part of the
performers.

Logically, homosexuals lead the most normal sex-life in prison.
They are usually found out and, unless they make a homosexual
friend among the guards, life can be very hard for them. Authority,
in the form of some senior officer or a junior guard, likes nothing
better than to punish a prisoner for some moral lapse. However,
homosexual prisoners seem able to meet almost at will, and they
often have the most favoured positions in gaol, usually because they
sell themselves to gain such positions.

Rupert noticed that the west Europeans, especially the Germans,
Danes and Dutch, were more prone to homosexuality. It is true
that to Russians, Slavs, Czechs and Balts homosexuality is quite
alien and Rupert encountered only one Hungarian male couple.

Alexander Berkman, an anarchist sentenced in 1892, who spent
twenty-two years in Russian prisons, wrote with compassion about
a young prisoner, Paul. "The youth was forced to work alongside a
man who persecuted and abused him because he resented improper
advances. Repeatedly Paul begged the governor to transfer him to
another department, but his appeals were ignored. The two prisoners
worked in the bakery. Early one morning, left alone, the man
attempted to violate the boy. In the struggle that followed the man
was killed. The prison management was determined to hang the
lad in the interests of discipline; the officers openly threatened that
that would fix his clock. Permission for a collection to engage a
lawyer was refused. Prisoners who spoke on the boy's behalf were
severely punished; the boy was completely isolated preparatory to
his trial, absolutely alone, helpless. However, some prisoners did
stand together and despite intimidation spoke the truth at the trial
and the boy was acquitted on the ground of self-defence."

To make another generalisation, from what little evidence there is,
homosexual tendencies are more marked among women politicals
than men. Elinor Lipper found that women prisoners had never
even heard of the existence of sexual relations between women and
learned about it for the first time as prisoners. In Miss Lipper's
experience lesbianism was relatively commonplace among female
prisoners.

Very few political prisoners have had an opportunity to associate with women, but where this has happened the women are sometimes more lustful than the men. There has been more than biological reason for this in Russia, where a woman captive having a baby can count on two years of comparative ease. Authority sees such children as sound raw material for Communism, so that for two years the mother is helped; then the child is taken away and the mother must return to her prison duties. When it is not possible for the women to reach the men some throw small bottles over the fence, in the hope that a co-operative man will give the means for an attempt at artificial insemination.*

In the Vorkuta prison camps there are—or were in recent years— ways of entering the women's compound. A woman cost 500 grams of bread, which any eager prisoner could save in a matter of days. Some men, the incident over, took half the bread back, saying that the experience was not worth 500 grams.

Ekart, in Kotlas during 1943-46, was appalled by the brutishness of sexual relations among men and women prisoners. He had never realised "how brutally a love scene could be enacted". Other prisoners say much the same thing. Thomsen, in various prisons in the Vorkuta district during the same period found the atmosphere one of "smut, eroticism and sexuality". Thomsen, a gynaecologist, found that in sexual excesses women could be a hundred times worse than men, but that usually they had sounder morals than male prisoners. Despite all pressure from male guards and officials as well as from prisoners, many women remain chaste.

When a woman is released from a remote prison or camp, especially in the lonely north or in Siberia, and has no means of reaching civilisation, she finds outside the prison several men waiting to propose marriage. Since no woman can live alone in these regions, she is obliged to take one of the ardent proposers in order to find shelter or protection, In any case, after long imprisonment she is afraid of independence and the decisions it will compel; marriage is an easy way out.

Thomsen, when head doctor in the surgical-gynaecological ward in Predshakhtana Camp in Vorkuta, fell in love with his assistant, Olite Priede, a Latvian fellow-prisoner who had been severely

* Rupert gives this and other related information in Chapter 8 of his book.

tortured in 1946 and condemned to death for supposedly belonging to the Latvian national resistance movement. The affair blossomed in the most unlikely surroundings and under great adversity. An enemy of Thomsen's had Olite put to labourer's work in the Arctic weather and the two were shunted to various labour camps, but they managed to meet occasionally and in 1950 Olite had a son; Thomsen was not to see the boy or Olite for six years. Repatriated to Denmark late in 1955, he worked for a year to have Olite and her child released and the two doctors were married in December, 1956.

Paul Ignotus had the rare experience of falling in love in prison and of conducting his love affair through sound signals and brief notes left in prison hiding places. His sweetheart, Florence, was in a cell on the floor above Ignotus' own in Gyujto Prison, Budapest. The difficult, frustrating courtship—they never set eyes on each other and never heard each other's voice—managed to succeed and Ignotus later married his girl, who had had, in some ways, a more severe captivity than his. Aged 43, she died in a London fire in 1968.

It would perhaps be more intellectually rewarding to study the sexual habits of the guards rather than of the prisoners. Many of them are sexually maladjusted and Ignotus says that all the warders he knew in various Hungarian gaols between 1949 and 1956 were oversexed. Warders, over-fed, bored and under-exercised, have plenty of time to indulge in flights of sexual fancy, a fact which some astute prisoners have used to their advantage. A captive with a gift for telling dirty stories or for making obscene sketches is certain of better treatment. Guards and even officers will give him paper and pencil to produce his masterpieces. Beatings and torturings are often mere manifestations of sexual intensity or perversion.

Under extreme conditions virility quickly deteriorates and pro-tracted imprisonment can impair it for many years after release. This aftermath is the essential tragedy of damage to a prisoner's sexual nature. The misery following lack of normal stimulation and fulfilment is acute enough in a man's earlier days in prison and in varying degrees is persistent throughout his imprisonment but it can become chronic and profound when he returns to normal life. When, with the means of natural stimulation and satisfaction within his reach, he finds himself unable to respond, he becomes even more bitter about his captivity.

12

Consolations: Poems, Letters

⚬⚬⚬⚬⚬⚬⚬⚬⚬⚬⚬⚬⚬⚬⚬⚬⚬⚬⚬⚬⚬⚬⚬⚬

That there can be any sort of consolation in a political prison may seem strange, but some prisoners have found deep compensation for their sufferings and most, though perhaps briefly, have found something to be grateful for, even if it is only the silence of a solitary cell. It is man's nature to seek for consolation and most adaptable men can rationalise benefits from their situation. Still, it would be inaccurate to give the impression that all such adaptability is merely rationalised; some of the letters which have survived seem to show a genuine conviction that imprisonment has its riches.

Many prisoners who go to prison well armoured with education and intellect in depth have their intellect sharpened. Pellico, in the early part of his imprisonment, found that his intellect became more acute simply because of the absence of distractions. Maroncelli, a friend of Pellico, developed such concentration that he was able to compose and memorise several thousand lyric and epic verses.

Political prisoners have often made the discovery that a situation lived through is never so bad in reality as in imagination. Those men who have faced a firing squad or other executioner only to be reprieved at the final moment have explained that being marched to the wall or the pinion-post was an anti-climax of fear much less acute than that of their imaginings during the previous days or weeks.

Begin says that a man should, in all circumstances, "give free rein to the thirst for knowledge which is in every man. Even if you are brought down to the depths of humiliation, to the valley of the shadow of death—open your eyes wide, and learn!" His argument is that as long as a man is learning, his inquisitors will not succeed in establishing between them and him the relationship they want and the prisoner maintains an equality with them. He advises the prisoner to "study" his persecutors. He will not then just be a "case", and from the knowledge that around him he can find material for study, he will draw strength to stand up to the test of degradation and remain a man.

Begin may be extravagant in his opinions but a richness of mind is certainly possible in prison. After a year, Rupert was aware that he had changed, in some ways, for the better. He speaks of a "new awareness", by which he means a more acute sensitivity to people and things, a finer responsiveness. "I even reached a state of peace of mind," he says.

Krishna Hutheesing puts it very simply, "It was after a spell in prison that one began to appreciate the value of the little things of life which one had before perhaps taken for granted." Yet she spent only a little over eleven months in gaol. She concedes, however, that political prisoners of the British in India were treated far better than political prisoners in other parts of the world.

One of Koestler's few compensations was "the wisdom of the Lord, who has so ordered the world that the day has only twenty-four hours and not twenty-five or thirty." He also found consolation in remembrance of a quotation from a book by Thomas Mann and which never failed him, though he does not reveal what it was.

In the Spielberg, Pellico was fortunate in having a number of serious books, by such authors as Virgil, Horace, Tacitus, Petrarch, Dante, Pascal, Racine, Schiller, Goethe, Shakespeare, Milton, Scott, and Byron. In this he was luckier than most other political prisoners, some of whom have spent years in prison without once seeing a printed word. Special dispensation is normally needed for a prisoner to be issued with a book.

Some prisoners report being allowed to keep a few personal belongings, such as pictures of wives and children, toothbrushes, toilet paper and perhaps a few cigarettes, but such concessions are rare and probably occur only when authority does not realise that such possessions greatly aid a man's morale.

Obviously, paper was permitted for those prisoners who wrote

poetry and letters, which by many devious means were preserved.
Only a selection is possible here.

Sir Thomas Wyatt, imprisoned for high treason in 1541, wrote a
pathetic little poem.

Epigram, 1541

Sighs are my food: drink are my tears,
Clinking of fetters such music would crave:
Stink and close air away my life wears:
Innocencie is all the hope I have.
Rain, wind or weather I judge by mine ears.
Malice assaulted that righteousness should have.
Sure I am Brian, this wound shall heal again,
But yet, alas, the scar shall still remain.

Ralph Chaplin, gaoled in 1917 for expressing anti-militaristic
opinions, also wrote a poem in prison.

Mourn not the Dead

Mourn not the dead that in the cool earth lie—
Dust unto dust—
The calm, sweet earth that mothers all who die
As all men must:

Mourn not your captive comrades who must dwell—
Too strong to strive—
Each in his steel-bound coffin of a cell,
Buried Alive;

But rather mourn the apathetic throng—
The cowed and the meek—
Who see the world's great anguish and its wrong
And dare not speak.

Erich Mühsom, a German revolutionary poet, was sentenced to
fifteen years in gaol for his part in the Bavarian Revolution of

1918. He served four years before being freed, and in 1934 was murdered by the Nazis in Oranienburg Prison Camp.

In the Cell

A day went shyly by—today as yesterday,
A quick and empty drop spilled into time.
When night out of her gathered folds
Strews her last shadow on the dawn's pale way,
The light's cold kiss no sweetness holds;
Tomorrow's face is but as yesterday's.

You grow not older—yet remain not young.
Habit awakes you and sends sleep to you.
You question never: How? No, only: When?
But When is future, When a challenge flung.
Woe be to you if habit kills your brain.
Unlearn not waiting. To yourself be true.

Prison

The waves are dancing on the sea
To the wind's free song.
The cell I have to dance in
Is ten feet long.

Longing trembles from the heavens
That makes hearts still.
My hole is dim with muddy glass
And barred with a grille.

Love with pale and gentle fingers
Softly marks a bed.
My door is made of iron:
To wooden planks I'm wed.

A thousand riddles, thousand questions
Make fools of those who try.
One only have I to answer:
Why I'm here? oh why?

Kurt Schwartz, about whom little is known, was a prisoner of the Nazi regime.

Five Steps: Moabit, 1934
Five steps forward, Five steps back,
So we go around.
You, man in front, you, man behind,
Don't speak aloud, speak low.

A warder here, a warder there,
Careful, let us not speak,
Have we not learned to understand
When our mouths are shut?

A warder here, a warder there,
Will not discourage us,
And are we caught, no force or fear
Will make our spirit break.

You man in front, you man behind,
We have much to say to each other,
Yet even when silently walking we know
That the future marches with us.

Alfred Schmidt-Sas, a teacher and musician, born in 1895, dedicated himself as an educator and agitator to the struggle against Nazism. He was imprisoned several times and on October 9, 1942, he was condemned to death by the People's Court and was executed in Plötzensee on April 9, 1943. Soon after his sentencing he wrote:

As in the game of chess, so too in life it matters not
Whether the duel be fought with pieces carved of wood
                                                    or gold
How one plays, and what one plays for, that alone
Reveals the man.

190

Whether, upon post-mortem, menials hurry off the corpse,
Or obsequies of state consign one to a splendid tomb,
How one dies, and what one dies for, that alone
Reveals the man.

From Plötzensee on Monday, March 8, 1943, he wrote, with manacled hands:

"Even those terrible minutes around one o'clock in the afternoon when they fetch the evening's victims from their cells and the whole house holds its breath, those minutes too are over for today, and this day can be chalked up as won . . . "

O strangely luminous life so close to death
Almost nine paces long
Is this my final whitened world?
Still nine days more, perhaps—
Then will fall
My head,
Which now still thinks and speaks and sees and hears.
The great sleep hovers very near,
With its dark pinion overshadowing
The blinding fire of wishes and of fears.
It mitigates the bitter, anguishful,
The longest moments of this human pain.
O strangely luminous life so close to death.

Divorced from the discipline of verse, prisoners' letters are often even more revealing. From the Tower, in July 1603, Raleigh wrote to his wife:

. . . That I can live never to see thee and my child more!—I cannot. I have desired God and disputed with my reason, but nature and compassion hath the victory. That I can live to think how you are both left a spoil to my enemies, and that my name shall be a dishonour to my child,—I cannot. I cannot endure the memory thereof. Unfortunate woman, unfortunate child . . .

. . . To witness that thou didst love me once, take care that thou marry not to please sense, but to avoid poverty, and to preserve thy child. That thou didst also love me living, witness it to others; to my poor daughter be charitable and teach thy son to love her for his father's sake . . .

I cannot live to think how I am derided, to think of the expectation of my enemies, the scorns I shall receive . . . O Death! destroy my memory which is my tormentor; my thoughts and my life cannot dwell in one body. But do thou forget me, poor wife, and thou mayst live to bring up my poor child . . .

I bless my poor child, and let him know his father was no traitor. Be bold of my innocence, for God—to whom I offer life and soul—knows it. And whosoever thou choose again after me, let him be thy beloved, for he is part of me and I live in him; and the difference is but in the number and not in the kind. And the Lord for ever keep thee and them, and give thee comfort in both worlds.

In 1839 William Lovett and John Collins, prominent Chartists, were gaoled for distributing a manifesto of protest against the police for using violence to break up a demonstration in Birmingham. They suffered severely in gaol but were in no mood to "confess" to any crime. The Secretary of State resorted to guile, but Lovett and Collins rejected his approach in a letter they wrote from Warwick Gaol on May 6, 1840.

The Visiting Magistrates of the County Gaol of Warwick having read to us a communication . . . in which it is stated that your lordship will recommend us to Her Majesty for a remission of the remaining part of our sentence, provided we are willing to enter into our own recognizances in £50 each for our good behaviour for one year, we respectfully submit the following as our answer: That to enter into any bond for our future misconduct would at once be an admission of past guilt; and, however a prejudiced jury may have determined the resolutions we caused to be published, condemnatory of the attack of the police, as an act in opposition to the law of libel, we cannot yet bring ourselves to believe that any guilt or criminality has been attached to our past conduct. We have, however, suffered the penalty of nearly ten months' imprisonment for having, in common with a large portion of the public press and a large majority of our countrymen, expressed that condemnatory opinion. We have been about the first political victims who have been classed and punished as misdemeanants and felons because we happened to be *of the working class*. We have had our health injured and our constitutions greatly undermined by the treatment already experienced, and we are disposed to suffer whatever future punishment may be inflicted upon us rather than enter into any such terms as those proposed by your lordship.

We remain your lordship's most obedient servants.

One of the most philosophical of all political prisoners was Rosa Luxemburg. Cultured, intelligent and passionate, she was in gaol in Berlin for a speech attacking military abuses. After her release she was again arrested in July, 1916, and held in "preventive detention" until November, 1918. In 1919 she was one of the Spartacist leaders and while under arrest was brutally murdered by some Prussian officers. From Wronke, on May 23, 1917, she wrote:

. . . Sonyusha, you are feeling embittered because of my long imprisonment. You ask: "How can human beings dare to decide the fate of their fellows? What is the meaning of it all?" You don't mind—I couldn't help laughing as I read. In Dostoyeffsky's [sic] *The Brothers Karamazoff*, one of the characters, Madame Hokhlakova, used to ask the same questions; she would look round from one member of the company to another, and would then blurt out a second question before there had been time to begin an answer to the first. My dear little bird, the whole history of civilisation (which according to a modest estimate extends through some twenty thousand years) is grounded upon "Human beings deciding the fate of their fellows"; the practice is deeply rooted in the material conditions of existence. Nothing but a further evolution, and a painful one, can change such things. At this hour we are living in the very chapter of the transition, and you ask "What is the meaning of it all?" Your query is not a reasonable one to make concerning the totality of life and its forms. Why are there blue-tits in the world? I really don't know, but I'm glad that there are, and it is sweet to me when a hasty "Zeezeebey" sounds suddenly from beyond the wall.

Another passionate woman revolutionary was Constance Markievicz, several times gaoled by the British for her Irish nationalist activities. From Holloway, probably in 1921, she wrote:

> . . . Don't bother about me here. As you know, the English ideal of modern civilisation always galled me. Endless relays of exquisite food and the eternal changing of costume bored me always to tears and I prefer my own to so many people's company. To make "conversation" to a bore through a long dinner-party is the climax of dullness. I don't mind hard beds or simple food: none of what you might call the "externals" worries me. I have my health and I can always find a way to give my dreams a living form. So I sit and dream and build up a world of birds and butterflies and flowers from the sheen in a dewdrop or the flash of a sea-gull's wing. Everyone who has anything to do with me is considerate and kind, and the only bore is being locked up, when there is so much to be done . . .

Jail is the only place where one gets time to read.

An interesting German prisoner was Ernst Toller, a notable poet who took a leading part in the Bavarian Revolution of 1919. He was later gaoled for five years and during this time he was able to write more freely than most politicals. From Niedershonenfeld in 1931 he wrote to Stefan Zweig about the maturing influence of prison.

> No, a man is not foolhardy who, himself at liberty, and free from care, praises his fate to a prisoner—so long as he desired the inner perfection of the prisoner. Because one would speak so only to a man whom one believes has spiritual strength enough to mature during his imprisonment. And I believe this strength has grown in me. Only the other day I wrote to Herr Tal, who, he tells me, is anxious to secure my release by the assistance of the German intellectuals, that, greatly touched as I was by his sympathy, I must ask him to abandon his plan. Tal fears that my creative powers will be damaged for life. I can't help smiling a little. We are living at a time when so many "would-be's" and "might-be's" are running around, men who lack any profound sense of compulsion, who can say either "Yes" or "Nay". It is about time that men voluntarily, from inescapable devotion, find the courage to live the ideas which they profess. That they see how essential such a life is. That they should give up thinking that life's meaning lies in making pictures of life.
>
> My fate seldom oppresses me, because I will it, have always

willed it—and I believe that I am secure against the danger of leaving the prison-house full of bitterness and resentment . . .

You say of Romain Rolland that he "loves humanity because he pities it rather than believes in it". This is, perhaps, the only constant and unembittered love. If belief be often disappointed, as it must be, it changes into enmity and bitterness and hatred of humanity.

Julius Leber, a Social Democrat and an enemy of the Nazis, was gaoled in Lübeck in 1933 and was another prisoner "happy" in captivity. His letter is philosophic but it must be remembered that at the time he was fairly well fed and that conditions were not too arduous.

At bottom life is beautiful only because of its tensions. Among my early "beautiful memories" I recall only a few rare occasions that gave me a joy as tense as that which fills me now in the expectation of your visit. And if that week goes by as rapidly as the present one, life will be nearly perfect. Yesterday when the inspector went through my cell and asked me how things were going, I could answer only that I am having a happy time under his administration. He thought I was crazy, of course. But this inward collectedness and concentration induced by confinement to the close quarters of a cell really creates a condition more auspicious for spiritual happiness than the dispersive haste of a free existence.

The situation is such that in this place each man must find his way, hold himself up, and develop strength by himself. "Here the heart is weighed in the balance; no one intercedes for him": this holds true here much more than on the battlefield. For here all pathos and high passion are lacking. Here the heart is put into the scale without any makeweight. Here one can delude oneself about nothing, absolutely nothing, for one is always alone within four bare walls that in the long months become as bright as a mirror of the soul.

Repeatedly, prisoners express the same sentiments about the spiritual, moral and intellectual solace of the cell. A priest, Pastor Paul Schneider, wrote from Coblenz in November 1937:

The life one lives here in one's cell is a very strange one. The external world is almost submerged. Whether it is winter or spring hardly concerns us. Even the events of national and international life have become remote; at least we look at them from a different, I might say a higher vantage point, thanks to the inward life that we are obliged to live and that allows us to look into our own souls, into God, and into eternity. This then is our evangelical monastic life, not self-chosen like that of the Catholics, but ordained for us by God for a time, which as such must be good and salutary for us.

Alfred Bösterli was a political prisoner in a different sense from most of the others in this book. A Swiss, he refused to register for military service some time during the 1920s and was imprisoned. In several letters to the War Resisters' International he made clear his rejection of the moral right of any political system to enforce military service on the public. Like so many others, Bösterli found satisfaction in his suffering.

Some people think one must vegetate in prison—like flowers in a cellar—white and wasted. It may be so for one who makes circumstances difficult for himself, who only complains over the injustice done to him, who has to suffer for his own wrong-doing. It is quite different for me, inwardly I am happy and cheerful. I even feel myself freer than outside, for a chain, and not the lightest, has been broken. The thought never comes, that perhaps after all I am wrong, and it would have been wiser to do as others. Naturally I am wrong as regards the law of man's making, but now I am free to follow an unwritten law, and this law is what every man bears in his breast.

So many people say to me: "What have you got from following this law? What help is it? You are only one—and there are so few—what good do you do?" I answer: "Has a farmer ever failed to sow, because he did not see at once the corn growing from the ground?" The silent hours in the cell have brought an experience which is more valuable than anything this varied world has to offer. Of course it does not happen so every day, nor all the time; but without consciously noticing it it is an inward experience.

Sentimental, emotional letters from political prisoners have been rarely found.* Perhaps letters written by prisoners of the Nazis would have been emotional, if only because of the natural self pity these

*This does not apply to prisoners of other types who have left much correspondence of this kind.

prisoners felt. But the vast majority were never permitted to write a letter.

Count Heinrich von Lehndorff-Steinort, an opponent of Hitler and the Nazis, was able to write, though with manacled hands, to his wife on the eve of his execution in September, 1944.

Most dearly beloved to me in all the world: This is probably the last letter you will receive from me on this earth. Although my thoughts have pursued an orbit around you day and night ever since our separation, and the contents of my heart could fill volumes, it becomes difficult nevertheless for me to write this letter. I fear that with everything I shall only pile a new burden upon your poor sorely tried heart. Nevertheless—you angel—your must hear and know everything about how I have lived, thought, and felt in the past weeks.

It is certain that, without having oneself lived through something of the sort, one imagines everything to be far worse than it really is when matters have become actual and there can be no more evading . . . My previous life is gradually sinking away altogether, and completely new standards prevail. With all that, you have of course certainly had your little joys, and I too have had moments of happiness. Only the causes for them have changed altogether. A kind word from a compassionate human being, permission to read or to smoke, to be able to walk a few steps across a sunny courtyard on being led to a hearing, and various little things like that make one exactly as happy as some great event or festive happening formerly did. Since I have been nearly always a little hungry, I have rejoiced as much over a piece of dry bread or over thin soup as I once did over a hunt dinner. And they are at least equally relished.

My beloved, I am picturing this for you in such detail so that you will not think that your Heini has spent these six weeks close to despair, staring at the walls of the cell, or pacing up and down like a captive animal in a cage. Please do not imagine this time to have been like that. Of course, one and only love, there have been also very sad and bitter hours, when my thoughts went their own way and I had to gather all my strength in order not to give way and to maintain composure. But I believe I succeeded. And even those hours were not purposeless, but surely necessary to lead me to the ground on which I stand now . . .

THE ANATOMY OF CAPTIVITY

A Jesuit, Alfred Delp, wrote many letters between his arrest on July 28, 1944 and his execution on February 2, 1945. Deeply disturbed by political evil, he had taken the dangerous step of working with a German underground resistance group. Even this man, a philosopher by inclination and by training, found that imprisonment deepened his existence.

My life now is of a strange sort. One becomes used to existence so quickly again, and is obliged now and then forcibly to recall the death sentence to consciousness. That is the peculiar thing about this death; the will to live remains unbroken, and every nerve is alive until hostile force overpowers all. Hence the usual omens and harbingers of death are absent in this situation. One of these days the door will open and the good warden will say, "Pack up, the car is coming in half an hour." The thing we have heard and experienced so often.

Up to now the Lord God has helped me most splendidly and kindly. I have not yet taken fright nor broken down. The hour of the flesh will no doubt strike too. Sometimes a sadness comes over me when I think of all that I still wanted to do. For it is only now that I have become a human being, inwardly free and far more genuine and more truthful, more real than before. Only now have my eyes acquired a flexibility of range enabling them to encompass all dimensions, and the normality needed to take in all perspectives. The contractions and atrophies are disappearing.

Shaved to the bone, all the intellectual, moral and spiritual stimulation and consolation professed by prisoners can be seen as a mere making the best of the situation. When the inevitable is recognised it becomes acceptable and can even be rationalised. There are so few moments of joy in the life of a political prisoner that they are magnified out of normal proportion. To a man kept in solitary confinement for years a mouse becomes an intimate friend. The happiness which prisoners write about should be regarded in this context. The privations of prison life can be, to some extent, beneficial. A fast for twenty-four hours can be healthy; being alone with his own company for a few days gives a man an opportunity for reappraisal; having no reading material for a short period can force the brain to use its own resources. But any of these can be dangerous in excess. Most of the men whose letters have survived

CONSOLATIONS: POEMS, LETTERS

knew they would be executed; having come to terms with death, the greatest problem of all, they could more easily find consolation in the time left to them and perhaps in knowing that they were martyrs of a type. But, realistically, there is no consolation in the life of a political prisoner, beyond the simple one which the honest Koestler found—the divine benevolence of there being twenty-four hours in a day, and not twenty-five.

Postscript

Primo Levi says of political captivity, "Our language lacks words to express this offence, the demolition of a man." He is speaking of the Italian but the observation applies to all tongues.

Yet from this demolition a prisoner can learn something, as Levi himself did. Heimler learned above all the value of freedom and life, that "all of us want peace, security, a life free from fear . . . we seek for the meaning of life and death . . . we cry for a woman on whose bosom we may rest our tormented head . . . Buchenwald taught me to be tolerant of myself, and by that means tolerant of others".

St. Paul, in his First Epistle to the Corinthians, says, "In all things we suffer tribulation, but we are not distressed; we are sore pressed, but we are not destitute; we endure persecution but we are not forsaken; we are cast down, but we do not perish . . . "

But not all political prisoners achieve such tolerance. Auchswitz gave birth to the proverb "When things change, they change for the worse".

If there is one thing about which all former prisoners agree, it is that sympathisers in the free world should express their sympathy. This contradicts the idea, which seems to be held by most people, that it is dangerous for the prisoner when outsiders take an interest in his case. Public indignation, whether at home or abroad, does impress authority sooner or later. It is easier to deal brutally with a forgotten man than with one who is the subject of appeals, protests and prayers. In any case, if words filter through to a prisoner that somebody is agitating on his behalf, it increases his morale. Amnesty's letter-writers, sending polite protests in shoals to Dictator or Minister for Justice, have shown how much can be achieved by such methods.

Relatively few can be actively helped, for political prisoners are numbered in hundreds of thousands, nearly all of them nameless, faceless and hopeless. And their numbers can only grow.

Bibliography

Beausobre, Iulia de, *The Woman Who Could Not Die*, Chatto and Windus 1938.

Begin, Menachem, *White Nights*, Macdonald 1957.

Bettelheim, Bruno, *The Informed Heart*, Free Press 1960, Thames & Hudson 1961.

Blumberg, Myrna, *White Madam*, Gollancz 1962.

Bone, Edith, *Seven Years Solitary*, Hamish Hamilton 1957, Harcourt 1957.

Burney, Christopher, *Solitary Confinement*, Burke 1952, Coward-McCann 1952.

Dreyfus, Alfred, *Five years of My Life*. Newnes 1901.

Gollwitzer, Helmut (Editor), *Dying We Live*, Harvill Press 1956, Pantheon 1956.

Gorbotov, Alexander, *Black Year*, Flegon Press 1954.

Ibarruri, Dolores, *They Shall Not Pass*, International Publications 1965, Lawrence & Wishart 1966.

Ignotus, Paul, *Political Prisoner*, Routledge & Kegan Paul 1959, Macmillan 1960.

Kirschen, Leonard, *Prisoner of Red Justice*, Barker 1963.

Koestler, Arthur, *Spanish Testament*, Gollancz 1937.

Levi, Primo, *If This is a Man*, Orion Press 1959, Bodley Head 1960.

Lipper, Elinor, *Eleven Years in Soviet Prison Camps*, Hollis and Carter 1951, Regnery 1951.

Malsagoff, S. A., *An Island Hell*, Philpot 1926.

Melgounov, S. P., *The Red Terror in Russia*, Lent 1926.

Mikes, George (Editor), *Prison, a Symposium*, Horizon 1963, Routledge & Kegan Paul 1963.

Paloczi-Horvath, George, *The Undefeated*, Little 1959, Secker and Warburg 1959.

Parvilahti, Unto, *Beria's Gardens*, Hutchinson 1959, Dutton 1960.

Pellico, Silvio, *My Prisons*, Oxford University Press 1963.

Pies, Otto, *The Victory of Father Karl*, Farrar, Strauss and Cudahy 1957, Gollancz 1957.

Popoff, George, *The Tcheka*, Philpot 1925.

Prychodko, Nicholas, *One of the Fifteen Million*, Dent 1952, Little 1952.

Rupert, Raphael, *A Hidden World*, Collins 1963, World 1963.

St. John Packe, Michael, *The Bombs of Orsini*, Secker and Warburg 1957.

Saloman, Ernst von, *The Captive*, Weidenfeld & Nicolson 1961.

Stock, A. G. and Reynolds, R. (Editors), *Prison Anthology*, Jarrolds 1938.

Thomsen, Alexander, *In the Name of Humanity*, Dutton 1963, Longmans 1963.

Turner, Henry, *International Incident*, Wingate 1956.

Vrba, Rudolph and Bestic, Alan, *I Cannot Forgive*, Sidgwick and Jackson 1963, Grove Press 1964.

Wells, Leon, *The Janowska Road*, Macmillan 1963, Cape 1966,

INDEX

205

Printed in Great Britain by John Gardner (Printers) Ltd.
Liverpool, 20

WARNER MEMORIAL LIBRARY
EASTERN COLLEGE
ST. DAVIDS, PA. 19087